# Learning Stati h

# StatTools

*A Guide to Statistics Using Excel and*
*Palisade's StatTools Software*

*Second Edition*

## S. Christian Albright

**Kelley School of Business**
**Indiana University**

*Published by:*

**Palisade Corporation**
**798 Cascadilla Street**

**Ithaca, NY 14850**

**(607) 277-8000**
**(607) 277-8001 (fax)**
**http://www.palisade.com (website)**
**sales@palisade.com (e-mail)**

# Table of Contents

**Chapter 1: Overview of StatTools**     1

1.1 Introduction ................................................................................... 1

1.2 Purpose of This Book ..................................................................... 3

**Chapter 2: Getting Started**     4

2.1 Introduction ................................................................................... 4

2.2 Loading StatTools ......................................................................... 4

2.3 Data Set Manager .......................................................................... 5

     Multiple Data Sets in a Workbook ...................................... 8

     No Variable Names ............................................................... 9

     Variables in Rows ............................................................... 10

     Multiple Ranges in a Data Set ........................................... 10

2.4 Stacked and Unstacked Data Sets ............................................ 12

2.5 Getting Data into Excel .............................................................. 13

     Importing from a Database ................................................ 16

     Importing from a Text File ................................................. 19

     Importing from the Web .................................................... 22

     Importing XML Data .......................................................... 24

2.6 Settings ....................................................................................... 26

     Settings For Each Analysis ................................................ 28

2.7 Getting Help ............................................................................... 29

**Chapter 3: Summary Statistics**     30

3.1 Introduction ................................................................................. 30

3.2 One-Variable Summary Statistics ............................................. 30

     Summary Statistics for Stacked Data with a Categorical Variable .. 33

     Summary Statistics for Multiple Data Sets ..................... 34

3.3 Correlation and Covariance ....................................................... 38

## Chapter 4: Summary Graphs                    **41**

4.1 Introduction ...................................................................41

4.2 Histograms ...................................................................41

4.3 Scatterplots ..................................................................47

4.4 Box-Whisker Plots .........................................................50

## Chapter 5: Statistical Inference             **53**

5.1 Introduction ...................................................................53

5.2 Confidence Intervals ......................................................53

Confidence Interval for a Mean or Standard Deviation ...................53

Confidence Interval for a Difference Between Means .....................56

Confidence Interval with Paired Samples ...................................60

Confidence Interval for a Proportion ........................................60

Confidence Interval for a Differences Between Proportions ..........60

5.3 Hypothesis Tests ..........................................................69

Test for a Mean or Standard Deviation ....................................69

Test for a Difference Between Means: Two-Sample Test ...............71

Test for a Difference Between Means: Paired-Sample Test.............72

Test for a Proportion ........................................................72

Test for a Difference Between Proportions .................................72

5.4 Sample Size Selection.....................................................77

Confidence Interval for a Mean ..............................................77

Confidence Interval for a Proportion.........................................78

Confidence Interval for Difference Between Means ......................79

Confidence Interval for Difference Between Proportions.................80

5.5 Analysis of Variance (ANOVA) .........................................82

One-Way ANOVA ..............................................................82

Two-Way ANOVA .............................................................82

5.6 Chi-Square Independence Test..........................................89

## Chapter 6: Normality Tests                   **92**

6.1 Introduction ...................................................................92

6.2 Chi-Square Test..............................................................92

6.3 Lilliefors Test.................................................................96

6.4 Q-Q Normal Plot ...........................................................98

## Chapter 7: Data Utilities                    **100**

7.1 Introduction ...................................................................100

7.2 Stacking and Unstacking Variables ....................................102

7.3 Transforming Variables....................................................106

7.4 Creating Dummy Variables ...............................................110

7.5 Creating Interaction Variables.................................................................113

7.6 Creating Combination Variables...............................................................115

7.7 Creating Lagged Variables and Difference Variables .................................117

7.8 Generating Random Samples ....................................................................120

**Chapter 8: Regression and Classification**                                    **122**

8.1 Introduction ..........................................................................................122

8.2 Regression ...........................................................................................122

      Stepwise Regression Procedures ..........................................................128

8.3 Logistic Regression ..............................................................................134

8.4 Discriminant Analysis ..........................................................................140

**Chapter 9: Time Series and Forecasting**                                     **146**

9.1 Introduction ..........................................................................................146

9.2 Time Series Graphs ...............................................................................146

9.3 Autocorrelation .....................................................................................150

9.4 Runs Test for Randomness .....................................................................152

9.5 Forecasting ...........................................................................................154

      Moving Averages ...............................................................................155

      Simple Exponential Smoothing ...........................................................160

      Holt's Method for Trend .....................................................................164

      Forecasting Seasonality......................................................................168

**Chapter 10: Quality Control**                                                **175**

10.1 Introduction ........................................................................................175

10.2 X-Bar Charts and R Charts....................................................................175

10.3 P Charts ..............................................................................................180

10.4 C Charts and U Charts..........................................................................184

**Chapter 11: Automating and Expanding StatTools**                            **189**

11.1 Introduction ........................................................................................191

11.2 Automating StatTools Procedures ........................................................191

11.3 Developing New Statistical Procedures .........**Error! Bookmark not defined.**

# Chapter 1: Overview of StatTools

## 1.1 Introduction

StatTools is a powerful and easy-to-use Microsoft Excel statistics add-in. It allows you to analyze data in Excel worksheets and work in the familiar Microsoft Office environment. By combining a powerful data manager, along with analyses that rival the best statistics packages available, StatTools brings you the best of two worlds: Excel's ease-of-use and reporting capabilities, and robust statistical power.

StatTools works just as Excel does, with tabs, ribbons, and custom worksheet functions, all inside Excel. Unlike stand-alone statistics software, there is no steep learning curve or upfront training costs with StatTools, because you work just as you are used to working in Excel. The data and variables are in Excel worksheets. You can utilize standard Excel formulas for calculations and transformations, along with Excel sorting and pivot tables. Reports and charts from your statistical analyses are in standard Excel format, so you can utilize all of Excel's built-in formatting capabilities.

StatTools replaces Excel's built-in statistical capabilities with its own robust and fast calculations. The accuracy of Excel's built-in statistical tools has often been questioned, and StatTools uses none of them. Even Excel's worksheet statistical functions are replaced by new, robust StatTools versions. For example, Excel's STDEV function is replaced by the StatTools StatSTDEV function. StatTools statistics calculations meet the highest tests for accuracy, with performance optimized through the use of C++ .DLLs, not macro calculations.

StatTools implements the most commonly used statistical procedures, and it also offers many capabilities for adding new, custom analyses. A total of 38 wide-ranging statistical procedures plus 8 built-in data utilities allow you to perform the most widely used statistical analyses, including descriptive statistics, normality tests, group comparisons, correlation, regression analysis, quality control, forecasting, and more.StatTools features live, "hot-linked" statistical calculations. When you change a value in Excel, you expect your worksheet to recalculate and give you new results. Many of the StatTools procedures behave in this same way. When you change a value in your data set, your statistical report automatically updates. To make this happen, StatTools enters formulas, not values, in the reports whenever it is feasible.

StatTools provides a comprehensive data set and variable manager in Excel, just as you would expect from a stand-alone statistics package. You can define any number of data sets, each with the variables you want to analyze, directly from your data in Excel. StatTools intelligently assesses your blocks of data, suggesting variable names and data locations for you. Your data sets and variables can reside in different workbooks and worksheets, allowing you to organize your data as you see fit. When you run statistical analyses, you can refer to your data sets instead of reselecting your data for each new statistical analysis. Also, StatTools variables are not limited in size to a single column of data in an Excel worksheet. For large data sets, you can use the same column across multiple worksheets for a single variable.

Excel is great for reports and graphs, and StatTools makes the most of this. StatTools uses Excel-formatted graphs, which can easily be customized for new colors, fonts, and added text. Report titles, number formats and text can be changed just as in any standard Excel worksheet. You can drag and drop tables and charts from StatTools reports straight into your own documents in other applications. Charts and tables stay linked to your data in Excel, so whenever your analysis reports change, your document automatically updates.

Excel has powerful data import features, so bringing your existing data into StatTools is easy. You can use standard Excel capabilities to read in data from Microsoft SQL Server, Oracle, Microsoft Access, or any other ODBC compliant database. You can also load data from text files or other applications. In general, if you can read data into Excel, you can use it with StatTools. StatTools saves all of its results and data in Excel workbooks. Just like any other Excel file, you can send your StatTools results and data to colleagues anywhere.

StatTools includes a complete object-oriented programming interface, where custom statistical procedures can be added using Excel's built-in VBA programming language. These custom procedures can utilize StatTools' built-in data management, charting and reporting tools, all accessible via StatTools custom controls, functions, and methods. Your custom procedures can even be displayed on the StatTools menu for easy access.

Even if you do not intend to write your own statistical procedures, you can use custom procedures written by others, right off the standard StatTools menu. You can simply copy a workbook with a new procedure into your PC's StatTools directory, and it will instantly appear on the StatTools Custom Analyses menu. When you run it, you will see all of the standard StatTools data management tools, combined with the new statistical analysis you need.

In short, StatTools fills a need many Excel users have expressed. It adds a comprehensive set of statistical tools to Excel's rather limited set, and it thereby enables all of you (not just the statistics experts) to perform statistical analyses in the environment where you are most comfortable—Excel.

## 1.2 Purpose of This Book

StatTools has plenty of online help, including an online reference manual. I do not intend to repeat this reference material here. Instead, I intend this to be a "mini statistics book" written around the StatTools add-in. In each chapter I discuss a logically grouped set of statistical procedures, grouped as they are in the StatTools menu structure. Each procedure is illustrated with a representative data set, explaining how StatTools can be used to analyze the data in an appropriate way. I make no attempt to explore every single feature that StatTools offers—this is best left to the reference manual. My goal here is to illustrate the most common statistical analyses, performed in the standard ways, and to show how StatTools implements these. I even discuss the meaning of the StatTools output, just for those of you who need a refresher in basic statistics. After many of the sections, I provide additional "notes" about alternative StatTools possibilities or statistical details.

In summary, this book is all about running statistical analyses properly, using the powerful StatTools add-in. It is not the step-by-step detailed description ("point your mouse to this button, click, and then click on OK") that accompanies many software packages. I assume you know how to do these simple things—and they are indeed simple with StatTools. My intent is instead to help you with the more difficult statistical issues: which statistical analysis to run and how to make sense of the output. Of course, all of this is done in the context of StatTools.

# Chapter 2: Getting Started

## 2.1 Introduction

StatTools is truly an easy software package to learn and use. However, like all software packages, you need to understand a few fundamental things about StatTools before you can use it properly. I will keep most of this chapter brief. The learning curve for StatTools is not at all steep, and I do not want to indicate otherwise with a lot of long-winded explanations. Nevertheless, I will spend some time in this chapter discussing a topic that actually has nothing to do with StatTools per se—namely, importing data into Excel so that StatTools can analyze it. This is clearly an important issue if the data set to be analyzed resides in a database, a text file, or some other location.

## 2.2 Loading StatTools

Always remember that StatTools is an Excel add-in. This means that StatTools cannot function on its own; it must function within Excel. As with any Excel add-in, there are two steps that you must follow to add it in: (1) you must install StatTools from the CD-ROM or the install file you downloaded from the Internet, and (2) you must load it into memory. The first step is explained in the instructions that come with the package. Basically, you install StatTools like you install any other Windows software. Of course, you need to perform this first step only once.

Once StatTools has been installed, you need to load it into memory. To do this, click on the Window Start button, locate the Palisade group in the list of programs, and select StatTools.

You will know that StatTools is loaded in memory when a StatTools tab with the ribbon shown in Figure 2.1 appears. As with other ribbons in Excel 2007, the items are grouped into categories, and each category has a number of dropdown menus with related menu items. I will discuss these throughout this book.

*Figure 2.1*

*StatTools Ribbon*

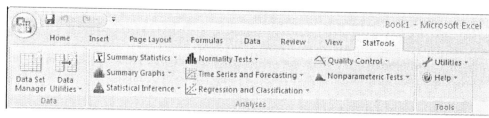

# 2.3 Data Set Manager

StatTools is built around the concept of a **data set**. To perform almost every statistical procedure within StatTools, you must first define a data set and then apply the procedure to this data set. Actually, once you have defined a data set, you can perform any number of statistical procedures on it; the data set needs to be defined only once. In fact, StatTools remembers it as a defined data set if you save the Excel file and reopen it later.

This data set concept is no different from most statistical packages. The almost universal concept of a data set (for statistical analysis) is a set of data in rows and columns, where the columns correspond to variables, usually with variable names at the tops of the columns, and the rows correspond to observations (or cases or records). A typical data set appears in Figure 2.2. There are three variables, labeled Person, Gender, and Salary, and there are 10 observations. Probably 99% of all data sets you will encounter look like this—data in a set of adjacent columns with variable names in the first row—and this is the StatTools default format. However, unlike many other statistical packages, StatTools allows other data set formats for the rare situations where they might be needed. I will discuss these other formats briefly below.

*Figure 2.2*

*Typical Data Set*

|    | A      | B      | C      |
|----|--------|--------|--------|
| 1  | Person | Gender | Salary |
| 2  | 1      | Female | 47000  |
| 3  | 2      | Male   | 57700  |
| 4  | 3      | Female | 72500  |
| 5  | 4      | Female | 40700  |
| 6  | 5      | Male   | 91800  |
| 7  | 6      | Male   | 28500  |
| 8  | 7      | Female | 52800  |
| 9  | 8      | Male   | 44000  |
| 10 | 9      | Male   | 42000  |
| 11 | 10     | Female | 36200  |

The first thing you will do in almost all StatTools statistical analyses is to define a set of data such as the one in Figure 2.2 as a StatTools data set. To do this, make sure the cursor is somewhere inside the data set and then select the **Data Set Manager** from the StatTools ribbon. (From here on in this book, all menu items refer to the StatTools ribbon.) If this is the first data set you are defining in this workbook, the message in Figure 2.3 will appear, which makes a guess at the range of data. This guess is usually correct, but you can override the address later on.

*Figure 2.3*

*Data Set
Message*

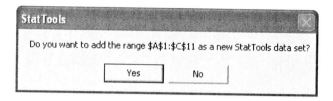

Click on Yes to bring up the dialog box in Figure 2.4. Here you can give the data set a more meaningful name if you like, you can override the range address, you can elect to apply cell formatting (for cosmetic purposes only), and you can specify the layout of the data. As mentioned earlier, the default layout, with variables in columns and variable names in the first row, is almost always the correct one.

*Figure 2.4*

*Data Set
Dialog Box*

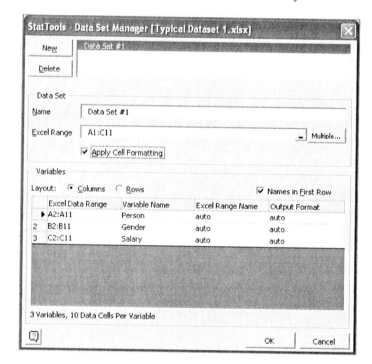

Assuming you check the Apply Cell Formatting option, the resulting data set is formatted as in Figure 2.5, with a blue background in the top row and some gridlines removed. More importantly, StatTools remembers this as a defined data set, with whatever name you chose for it. In fact, if you select the **Data Set Manager** menu item again, the dialog box appears as in Figure 2.6. At this point, you could delete this data set (not the data, just the definition of the data set), or you could change its settings. Note how StatTools gives Excel range names to the data ranges for the variables, according to its own conventions. For example, the salaries in the range C2:C11 receive the range name ST_Salary. You can change these range names if you really want to, but I recommend that you leave them alone. StatTools uses them for its own purposes, such as in formulas for the statistical output, so any changes could have undesired consequences.

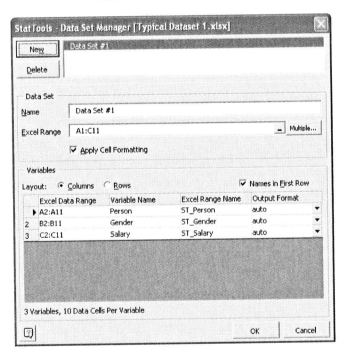

*Figure 2.5*

*Formatted Data Set*

*Figure 2.6*

*Data Set Dialog Box with Range Names*

The variables in a data set do not necessarily need to have equal lengths. As an example, the data in Figure 2.7 could result from asking random samples of 13 males and 10 females for their ratings of some product. If you define a data set for these data, StatTools will use the entire rectangular range A1:B14, and it will treat the cells B12 through B14 as missing. (This is a typical example of unstacked data, which StatTools is perfectly able to accommodate. I will discuss stacked and unstacked data in later chapters.)

Figure 2.7

Data Set
with
Unequal
Variable
Lengths

| | A | B |
|---|---|---|
| 1 | Male Ratings | Female Ratings |
| 2 | 6 | 2 |
| 3 | 5 | 3 |
| 4 | 5 | 4 |
| 5 | 9 | 6 |
| 6 | 3 | 1 |
| 7 | 8 | 10 |
| 8 | 9 | 3 |
| 9 | 9 | 9 |
| 10 | 1 | 3 |
| 11 | 1 | 10 |
| 12 | 10 | |
| 13 | 4 | |
| 14 | 4 | |

If you work with a single data set per workbook, with variables in adjacent columns and variable names in the top row—the situation most people encounter in most of their statistical analyses—then you can stop reading this section right now. You understand all you need to understand about StatTools data sets. However, StatTools allows several alternatives for the cases that do not conform to this setup. I discuss them briefly in the remainder of this section.

## Multiple Data Sets in a Workbook

StatTools allows you to have multiple data sets in a single workbook, even in a single worksheet, and these data sets could be related or totally unrelated. For example, consider the data in Figure 2.8. I first defined a data set, with default name Data Set #1, for the data in columns A–C. Then I went through the same menu to define a second data set, with default name Data Set #2, for the data in columns E–F. Although these might both correspond to the same 10 people, you can now work with them independently. When you run a statistical analysis, StatTools allows you to choose which of the defined data sets to work with.

Figure 2.8

Multiple
Data Sets

| | A | B | C | D | E | F |
|---|---|---|---|---|---|---|
| 1 | Person | Gender | Salary | | Person | Age |
| 2 | 1 | Female | 47000 | | 1 | 30 |
| 3 | 2 | Male | 57700 | | 2 | 56 |
| 4 | 3 | Female | 72500 | | 3 | 43 |
| 5 | 4 | Female | 40700 | | 4 | 53 |
| 6 | 5 | Male | 91800 | | 5 | 33 |
| 7 | 6 | Male | 28500 | | 6 | 45 |
| 8 | 7 | Female | 52800 | | 7 | 56 |
| 9 | 8 | Male | 44000 | | 8 | 53 |
| 10 | 9 | Male | 42000 | | 9 | 47 |
| 11 | 10 | Female | 36200 | | 10 | 35 |

## No Variable Names

It is also possible, but not recommended, to define a data set without variable names in the top row, as in Figure 2.9. However, when you fill in the Data Set Manager dialog box in Figure 2.10, you must uncheck the Names in First Row option, and you must type in your own variable names in the Variables section. So one way or the other, a defined data set must have variable names.

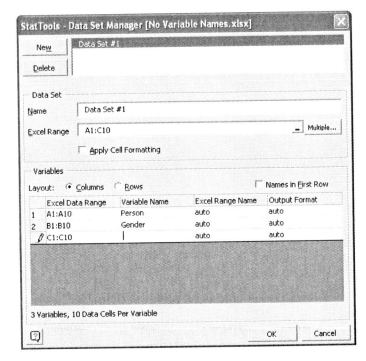

*Figure 2.9*

*Data Set with No Variable Names*

*Figure 2.10*

*Supplying Variable Names*

## Variables in Rows

It is standard statistical convention to put variables in columns and observations in rows. However, StatTools allows you to reverse this for the rare situation where you have a data set as in Figure 2.11. The only change required is to check the Rows option for the layout in the Data Set Manager dialog box.

*Figure 2.11*

*Variables in Rows*

| | A | B | C | D | E | F | G | H | I | J | K |
|---|---|---|---|---|---|---|---|---|---|---|---|
| 1 | Person | 1 | 2 | 3 | 4 | 5 | 6 | 7 | 8 | 9 | 10 |
| 2 | Gender | Female | Male | Female | Female | Male | Male | Female | Male | Male | Female |
| 3 | Salary | 47000 | 57700 | 72500 | 40700 | 91800 | 28500 | 52800 | 44000 | 42000 | 36200 |

## Multiple Ranges in a Data Set

StatTools allows you to spread out a data set over multiple ranges, even over multiple worksheets within the same workbook. This is especially useful when you have really large data sets. For example, consider the data on 2000 people in Figures 2.12 and 2.13. The first 1000 observations are on one sheet, and the second 1000 are on another sheet. You could copy the data on persons 1001–2000 to the first sheet, so that you have all of the data together, but this is not necessary.

*Figure 2.12*

*First Part of Data Set*

| | A | B | C |
|---|---|---|---|
| 1 | Person | Gender | Salary |
| 2 | 1 | Female | 47000 |
| 3 | 2 | Male | 57700 |
| 4 | 3 | Female | 72500 |
| 5 | 4 | Female | 40700 |
| 6 | 5 | Male | 91800 |
| 7 | 6 | Male | 28500 |
| 8 | 7 | Female | 52800 |
| 999 | 998 | Male | 35200 |
| 1000 | 999 | Female | 58700 |
| 1001 | 1000 | Female | 54100 |

*Figure 2.13*

*Second Part of Data Set*

| | A | B | C |
|---|---|---|---|
| 1 | Person | Gender | Salary |
| 2 | 1001 | Male | 44600 |
| 3 | 1002 | Male | 62500 |
| 4 | 1003 | Male | 48700 |
| 5 | 1004 | Female | 58600 |
| 6 | 1005 | Male | 49100 |
| 7 | 1006 | Male | 21400 |
| 8 | 1007 | Female | 45000 |
| 999 | 1998 | Male | 36300 |
| 1000 | 1999 | Male | 56700 |
| 1001 | 2000 | Male | 49600 |

To create one combined data set for these data, put your cursor somewhere in the data in the first sheet and select **Data Set Manager**. The key now is to click on the Multiple button in Figure 2.14 to bring up the dialog box in Figure 2.15. Here, you can select multiple ranges. To do so, select a new row in this dialog box (we selected the second row), click on the Select button, and drag the second range. If there are variable names at the top of each range, as we have here, make sure the bottom option in this dialog box is checked. The result is a large data set spread over two sheets that works like a usual one-sheet data set.

*Figure 2.14*

*Data Set Manager Dialog Box*

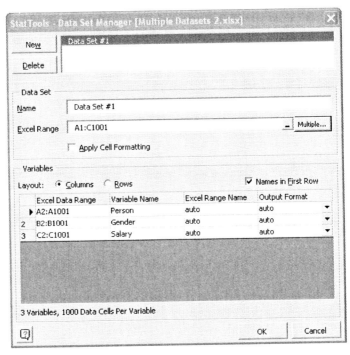

*Figure 2.15*

*Specifying Multiple Ranges*

As Figure 2.115 indicates, you can have many ranges (not just two) in a single data set. This allows you to analyze extremely large data sets. Of course, with over a million rows available in an Excel 2007 worksheet, there is less need than in previous versions of Excel to spread large data sets over multiple worksheets (or workbooks), but StatTools still enables you to do so.

# 2.4 Stacked and Unstacked Data Sets

There are two basic formats for data sets, stacked and unstacked, and you need to understand the difference between them for many of the statistical analyses you will perform. Typically, the difference is important if your data set has at least one categorical variable, such as gender, and you want to compare statistics of some other variable, such as exam score, across the different categories. Then the essential difference between stacked and unstacked formats appears in Figures 2.16 and 2.17.

*Figure 2.16*

***Stacked Data***

| | A | B | C |
|---|---|---|---|
| 1 | Person | Gender | Exam score |
| 2 | 1 | Female | 82 |
| 3 | 2 | Female | 88 |
| 4 | 3 | Male | 74 |
| 5 | 4 | Male | 97 |
| 6 | 5 | Male | 83 |
| 7 | 6 | Male | 96 |
| 8 | 7 | Female | 75 |
| 9 | 8 | Male | 86 |
| 10 | 9 | Male | 69 |
| 11 | 10 | Female | 86 |

*Figure 2.17*

***Unstacked Data***

| | A | B |
|---|---|---|
| 1 | Male exam score | Female exam score |
| 2 | 92 | 71 |
| 3 | 89 | 100 |
| 4 | 82 | 92 |
| 5 | 81 | 73 |
| 6 | 86 | 88 |
| 7 | 72 | 66 |
| 8 | 86 | |
| 9 | 66 | |

In Figure 2.16, the exam scores for males and females are stacked on top of one another in a single column. Of course, the Gender column indicates which scores are for males and which are for females. In contrast, there are two separate exam score columns for the unstacked data in Figure 2.17, one for males and one for females. In this case, there is no requirement that the two column lengths be equal.

In many analyses, StatTools lets you choose what type of data format you have through the **Format** button illustrated in Figure 2.18 for the data set in Figure 2.16. If you check the Stacked option, you get two columns of checkboxes for choosing variables: a **Cat** list (for category) and a **Val** list (for value). The meaning is simple: In this case, you want to compare exam scores across gender.

**Figure 2.18**

*Cat and Val Variables*

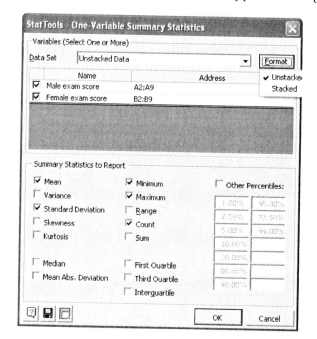

On the other hand, you could do the same comparison across genders for the data in Figure 2.17. In this case, the correct options would appear as in Figure 2.19.

**Figure 2.19**

*Dialog Box for Unstacked Data*

Again, this issue of stacked versus unstacked is relevant only when you are comparing some "value" variable, such as exam score, across categories. If you are not comparing across categories, stacked versus unstacked is an irrelevant issue.

# 2.5 Getting Data into Excel

The data you need to analyze do not always reside in an Excel worksheet. Excel has tools for importing external data and we discuss the most important of them in this section. Keep in mind that this section has nothing to do with StatTools per se, but StatTools does you little good if you can't get your data into Excel in the first place.

## Importing from a Database

Database packages such as Microsoft Access, Microsoft SQL Server, and Oracle are well-suited to storing data and querying data. This is why so much data is stored in database systems, usually in relational form. (This section assumes that you know the basics of relational databases, including tables, relations, primary and foreign keys, and queries.) However, database systems are not good at analyzing data. Therefore, it is common to import data from a database into Excel for statistical analysis.

Microsoft and other companies have recognized this need and have developed standards for "talking to" databases through a common language, whether the database package is Access, SQL Server, Oracle, or others. This means you need to know very little about any particular database package. All you need to know is how the data are structured (table names, field names, keys, and relationships) to get Excel to import the data you need.

This is a rather large topic, so I will only outline the steps required and then illustrate them for an Access database. The basic steps, regardless of the source database package, are to:

1. Create a connection to the database, possibly over a network,
2. Create and run a query to get exactly the data you want, and
3. Return the query results to Excel.

This is all done through Excel, along with Microsoft Query, a component of the Microsoft Office suite.

The details of step 1 vary from one database package to another and are be covered here. For example, if you are trying to import SQL Server data from your company's database server, you will have to supply a server name, along with a username and password. However, if the database is an Access database that resides on your hard drive, as I will illustrate here, then creating the connection is just about as easy as opening a file.

To illustrate the procedure, consider the Access database in the file **SalesOrders.mdb**. It has a set of related tables for a company that sells its products to various customers. The structure of the database is fairly self-explanatory and appears in Figure 2.20. Customers place orders, each order can be for multiple products, and the products are classified into various categories. The objective is to import selected data into Excel.

*Figure 2.20*

***Structure of SalesOrder Database***

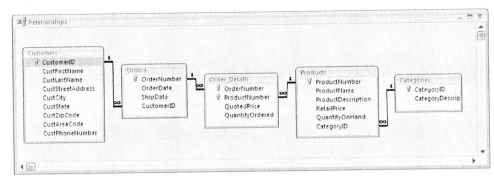

First, note that you need only the database file and the information in Figure 2.20 to do this. You do not need to open Access. In fact, Access doesn't even need to be installed on your PC. To import the data, select the **From Microsoft Query** item from the **From Other Sources** dropdown on Excel's Data ribbon. This launches Microsoft Query and brings up the dialog box in Figure 2.21. Select the <New Data Source> item and click on OK. (I typically uncheck the bottom box because I don't like to use the Query Wizard.) This brings up the dialog box in Figure 2.22 where you can define and establish a connection to the SalesOrder database. In this dialog box, enter any descriptive name in the first box, select the Microsoft Access Driver from the dropdown list in the second box, and click on the Connect button. This takes you to a screen where you can browse for the **SalesOrder.mdb** file. (The location of the file on my PC appears next to the Connect button.)

*Figure 2.21*

***Choose Data Source Dialog Box***

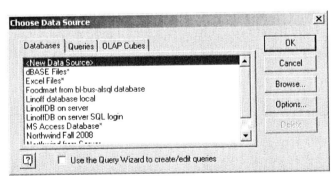

*Figure 2.22*

*Connection
Information*

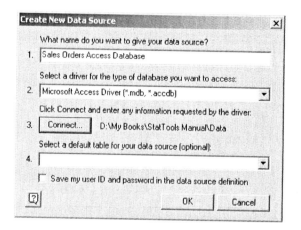

This is all the information required to establish a connection to the database, so when you click on OK, you get to define your query — that is, specify the data you want to return to Excel. I won't discuss all of the details (which are quite straightforward), but I show one possible query and the results of it in Figure 2.3. Here I am requesting all of the fields listed in the bottom pane for all orders placed from August 1, 1999 on.

*Figure 2.23*

*Query and
Query
Results*

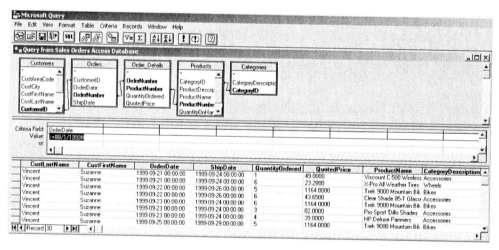

At this point you are still in Microsoft Query. To return the results to Excel, select Microsoft Query's **File->Return Data to Microsoft Excel** menu item and select the Table format. The data are imported nicely, field names and all, into an Excel table. In fact, Excel even retains a link to the Access data, so that if the latter changes, the data in Excel can easily be refreshed by a click of a button. (To do so, select Excel's **Refresh All** button on the Data ribbon.)

## Importing from a Text File

Text files, sometimes called ASCII files, are a common source of data. The reason is that they represent the "lowest common denominator"—virtually every type of software package can read text files. A text file is basically a single-table database, where each line typically contains an value for each variable. The variable names might or might not be in the top line. The data in a given line are either in fixed-width or variable-width format. You can think of fixed-width format as one where the columns are lined up nicely. For example, variable 1 might be stored in columns 1–6, variable 2 might be stored in columns 7–10, and so on.

Fixed-width format used to be more common than it is today. It is probably more common today to see variable-width format, with delimiters separating the pieces of data. The most common delimiters are tabs, spaces, and commas. For example, a typical line in a comma-delimited file might look like:

**342,Male,97250**

One advantage of text files is that you can open them in a text editor such as Notepad. So if someone sends you data in a text file, you can use Notepad to examine its structure to determine if it is in fixed-width format or is, say, comma-delimited. This will help you import the data more easily into Excel.

To illustrate the process, I will import the data from the sample file **TextFile.txt**, shown in Figure 2.24. This is a comma-delimited file. Note the two consecutive commas for person 5. These are used to indicate that this person's gender is unknown.

*Figure 2.24*

*Text File Data in Notepad*

To import this data set into Excel, select **From Text** on Excel's Data ribbon and locate the file in the usual way, making sure to specify the correct file type in the bottom dropdown list, as in Figure 2.25. This launches a 3-step wizard. In the first step, shown in Figure 2.26, make sure the Delimited option is selected. In the second step, shown in Figure 2.27, make sure Comma is selected as the delimiter. (In this step you can also verify that the row for person 5 is being handled correctly.) The third step, not shown, lets you make some optional choices that we don't need here.

*Figure 2.25*

*Open File
Dialog Box*

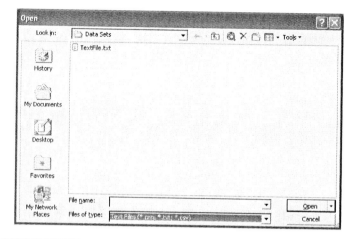

*Figure 2.26*

*Step 1 of
Import
Wizard*

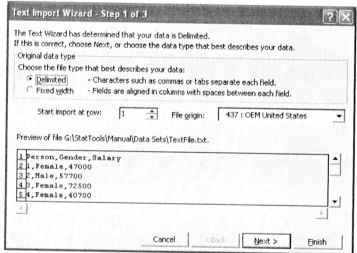

Figure 2.27

Step 2 of
Import
Wizard

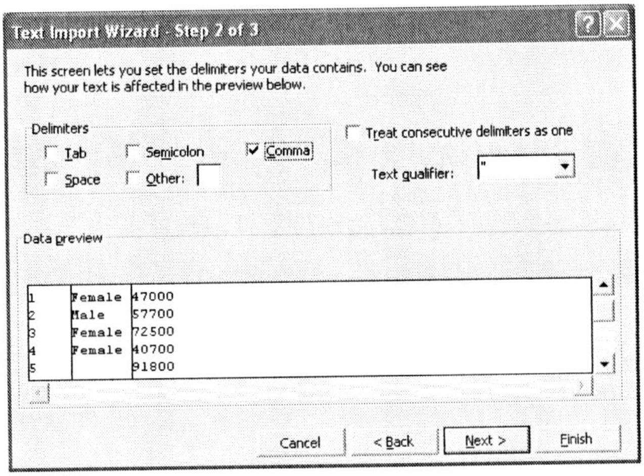

**Text Import Wizard - Step 2 of 3**

This screen lets you set the delimiters your data contains. You can see how your text is affected in the preview below.

Delimiters
- [ ] Tab
- [ ] Space
- [ ] Semicolon
- [ ] Other:
- [✓] Comma

[ ] Treat consecutive delimiters as one

Text qualifier: "

Data preview

| 1 | Female | 47000 |
| 2 | Male | 57700 |
| 3 | Female | 72500 |
| 4 | Female | 40700 |
| 5 | | 91800 |

Cancel    < Back    Next >    Finish

The imported data appear in Figure 2.28. It is important to scan the results visually, especially to ensure that everything lines up in the correct columns. It can be dangerous to *assume* that Excel always gets it right—as we and many of our colleagues have discovered when working with large and messy data sets!

Figure 2.28

Imported
Data in
Excel

| | A | B | C |
|---|---|---|---|
| 1 | Person | Gender | Salary |
| 2 | 1 | Female | 47000 |
| 3 | 2 | Male | 57700 |
| 4 | 3 | Female | 72500 |
| 5 | 4 | Female | 40700 |
| 6 | 5 | | 91800 |
| 7 | 6 | Male | 28500 |
| 8 | 7 | Female | 52800 |
| 9 | 8 | Male | 44000 |
| 10 | 9 | Male | 42000 |
| 11 | 10 | Female | 36200 |

## Importing from the Web

The Web is becoming *the* place to find information, including data sets appropriate for statistical analysis. Fortunately, Excel has a Web query tool for importing Web data. This tool has improved as each new version of Excel has appeared, and it will probably continue to improve. If nothing else, it will almost certainly change, and any exact step-by-step directions provided here will probably have to be modified in future versions of Excel. With that said, I will describe briefly how Web queries now work (in Excel 2007).

As you probably know, Web pages are written in HTML, a markup language that uses a variety of tags to format the pages. One of the more important tags is the <Table> tag. These <Table> tags are used to format tables of data, and they are also used to line things up. Therefore, <Table> tags sometimes indicate real "tables," and sometimes they indicate items that bear no resemblance to tables. In any case, Excel's Web query tool lets you go to a Web page and locate all elements with <Table> tags. You can then decide which of these to import into Excel.

To illustrate, I experimented with a Yahoo site that allows me to find historical stock prices for any company (designated by its ticker symbol) and selected dates. A typical URL at this site is:

http://finance.yahoo.com/q/hp?s=IBM&a=0&b=1&c=2000&d=6&e=1&f=2003&g=m

I got this particular URL by going to the base site and filling in the Yahoo form in Figure 2.29.

*Figure 2.29*

*Yahoo Form*

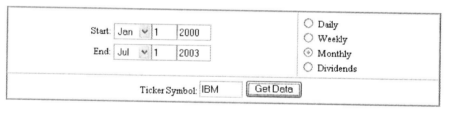

Once you have found a URL that takes you to data you want to import, open Excel and select **From Web** from the Data ribbon. This opens the dialog box in Figure 2.30. You need to enter (or paste) your URL into the top Address box and click on Go. This opens the Web page and indicates all "tables" with a yellow arrow box. You can select any of these that you want to import, as I have done in the table toward the bottom. (The arrow becomes a green check once it is selected.)

Figure 2.30

Excel Web
Query
Dialog Box

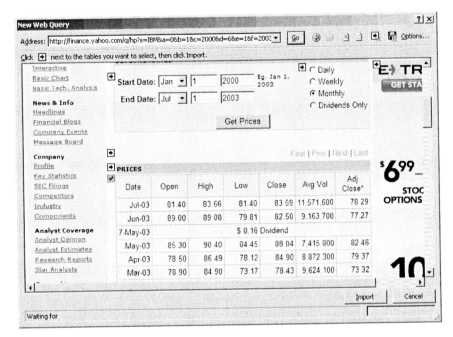

The imported data from this table appear in Figure 2.31. Typically, you must keep your fingers crossed and hope that you get what you want, formatted in a decent way. There aren't many strict rules out on the Web, so you sometimes have to experiment to get the desired data. Note that Excel retains a link to the Web data, so that if the latter changes, you can easily refresh the imported data with a click of a button. (To do so, select **Refresh All** from the Data ribbon.)

Figure 2.31

Imported
Data

| | A | B | C | D | E | F | G |
|---|---|---|---|---|---|---|---|
| 1 | Date | Open | High | Low | Close | Avg Vol | Adj Close* |
| 2 | | 3-Jul | 81.4 | 83.66 | 81.4 | 83.59 | 11,571,600 | 78.29 |
| 3 | | 3-Jun | 89 | 89.08 | 79.81 | 82.5 | 9,163,700 | 77.27 |
| 4 | 7-May-03 $ 0.16 Dividend | | | | | | |
| 5 | | 3-May | 85.3 | 90.4 | 84.45 | 88.04 | 7,415,800 | 82.46 |
| 6 | | 3-Apr | 78.5 | 86.49 | 78.12 | 84.9 | 8,872,300 | 79.37 |
| 7 | | 3-Mar | 78.9 | 84.9 | 73.17 | 78.43 | 9,624,100 | 73.32 |
| 8 | 6-Feb-03 $ 0.15 Dividend | | | | | | |
| 9 | | 3-Feb | 78.2 | 80.05 | 74.31 | 77.95 | 8,013,500 | 72.87 |
| 10 | | 3-Jan | 78.8 | 88.95 | 77.02 | 78.2 | 9,698,900 | 72.96 |
| 11 | | 2-Dec | 88.6 | 89.46 | 75.6 | 77.5 | 7,592,100 | 72.31 |
| 12 | 6-Nov-02 $ 0.15 Dividend | | | | | | |
| 13 | | 2-Nov | 78.9 | 88.11 | 76.7 | 86.92 | 9,370,900 | 81.1 |
| 14 | | 2-Oct | 59.2 | 79.79 | 54.01 | 78.94 | 12,847,400 | 73.52 |
| 15 | | 2-Sep | 74.2 | 77.5 | 57.99 | 58.31 | 9,934,200 | 54.31 |

## Importing XML Data

If you are doing your best to keep up in today's fast-moving world of technology, you have probably heard of XML. Like HTML, XML is a markup language, but it has the advantage that you can create your own self-documenting tags. Therefore, the structure of an XML file conveys, in a fairly self-explanatory way, what the data mean. Besides this self-documenting feature, the main advantage of using XML files for storing data is they are plain text files. This means they can be distributed easily over a network and can be read by virtually any computer system that receives them. For this reason, they are quickly becoming *the* means of distributing data. In addition, as new versions of Excel appear, their most important changes tend to be in their improved ability to work with XML data. (You are probably not aware of it, but starting in Excel 2007, your Excel spreadsheets are actually stored in XML format.)

If you have never seen XML data, hang on. As we show in Figure 2.32, it is not a pretty sight! This is a portion of an XML file called **Orders.xml**. I obtained this screen shot by opening the file in Internet Explorer. An XML file is always structured in a hierarchical fashion. This particular file stores information on orders. So inside each <Orders> tag, there are tags for the various pieces of information about the order, as well as the information itself.

*Figure 2.32*

*Portion of XML Data File*

```
<?xml version="1.0" encoding="UTF-8" ?>
 - <dataroot xmlns:od="urn:schemas-microsoft-com:officedata">
  - <Orders>
     <OrderID>10248</OrderID>
     <CustomerID>WILMK</CustomerID>
     <EmployeeID HomeOffice="US">5</EmployeeID>
     <OrderDate>1996-07-04T00:00:00</OrderDate>
     <RequiredDate>1996-08-01T00:00:00</RequiredDate>
     <ShippedDate>1996-07-16T00:00:00</ShippedDate>
     <ShipVia>3</ShipVia>
     <Freight>32.38</Freight>
     <ShipName>Vins et alcools Chevalier</ShipName>
    - <ShipAddress>
       <![CDATA[ 59 rue de l'Abbaye  ]]>
     </ShipAddress>
     <ShipCity>Reims</ShipCity>
     <ShipPostalCode>51100</ShipPostalCode>
     <ShipCountry>France</ShipCountry>
   </Orders>
```

Fortunately, it is easy to import XML data into Excel. All you need to do is open the file in the usual way, making sure to designate the file type as XML. There are not even any wizards to go through. A portion of the imported data from the **Orders.xml** file appears in Figure 2.33. As this figure illustrates, the data is imported as an Excel table.

*Figure 2.33*

*Imported
Excel Data*

| | A | B | C | D | E | F |
|---|---|---|---|---|---|---|
| 1 | OrderID ▼ | CustomerID ▼ | EmployeeID ▼ | HomeOffice ▼ | OrderDate ▼ | RequiredDate ▼ |
| 2 | 10248 | WILMK | 5 | US | 7/4/1996 0:00 | 8/1/1996 0:00 |
| 3 | 10249 | TRADH | 6 | US | 7/5/1996 0:00 | 8/16/1996 0:00 |
| 4 | 10250 | HANAR | 4 | US | 7/8/1996 0:00 | 8/5/1996 0:00 |
| 5 | 10251 | VICTE | 3 | US | 7/8/1996 0:00 | 8/5/1996 0:00 |
| 6 | 10252 | SUPRD | 4 | US | 7/9/1996 0:00 | 8/6/1996 0:00 |
| 7 | 10253 | HANAR | 3 | US | 7/10/1996 0:00 | 7/24/1996 0:00 |
| 8 | 10254 | CHOPS | 5 | US | 7/11/1996 0:00 | 8/8/1996 0:00 |
| 9 | 10255 | RICSU | 9 | US | 7/12/1996 0:00 | 8/9/1996 0:00 |
| 10 | 10256 | WELLI | 3 | US | 7/15/1996 0:00 | 8/12/1996 0:00 |
| 11 | 10257 | HILAA | 4 | US | 7/16/1996 0:00 | 8/13/1996 0:00 |

# 2.6 Application Settings

Unlike many statistical packages that are fairly rigid in what they allow you to do, StatTools provides a number of options. Basically, this is because StatTools resides within Excel, and Excel allows you to do just about anything. StatTools provides some of its options in an Application Settings menu item, where you can choose how you want it to operate. For example, you can choose where you typically want your output reports to be placed. The chances are that you will choose your favorite settings once and never change them again. However, you are allowed to change them at any time, so that your revised settings will be in force for the current analysis or for future analyses.

To choose settings, select the **Application Settings** item from the Utilities (not *Data* Utilities) dropdown. (Starting with version 5.0 of its DecisionTools Suite, Palisade provides a similar Utilities dropdown with an Application Settings item for each of its add-ins.) This brings up the dialog box in Figure 2.34 with several groups of settings: General Settings, Reports, Utilities, Data Set Defaults, and Analyses.

*Figure 2.34*

*Application Settings*

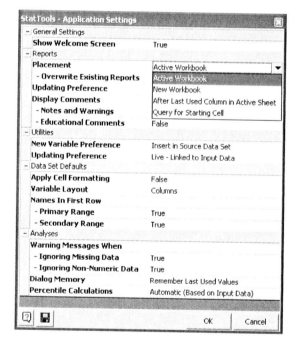

The setting you will probably change most often is the Placement setting in the Reports group. This lets you choose where to place your StatTools output reports. As shown in Figure 2.34, the four possibilities are: (1) in a new worksheet in the current (active) workbook, (2) in a newly created Report workbook, (3) to the right of the data in the current (active) worksheet, and (4) in a location of your choice (where you specify the top-left cell of this output range). I tend alternate between options (1) and (4), but the choice is up to you.

Besides the placement of the report, you can check whether you want the output to be live—linked to the original data through Excel formulas—or static, with numbers only. I prefer the "live" option. (Note, however, that there are a few procedures, notably regression, where the output is static regardless of the option you choose here.) You can also choose to enter either of two types of comments in output cells. These cell comments provide help on the meaning of certain statistical outputs, so unless you find the red comment marks in cells annoying, I recommend that you ask for them.

The Utilities group in Figure 2.34 is useful for the data utilities StatTools provides. These are discussed in detail in Chapter 7, as well as the settings in Figure 2.34, so I will postpone their discussion until then. However, the default settings shown here are probably the ones you will want.

The Data Set Defaults group in Figure 2.34 lets you choose a few settings for the data set manager that was discussed in Section 2.3. I recommend the settings shown here. Using them, the data set manager will always assume, for example, that you do not want to apply cell formatting to your data sets and that your variables are in columns with names in the top row. There is no harm in letting the data set manager make these assumptions because you can always override them when you define a particular data set.

Finally, the Analyses group in Figure 2.34 is one you will appreciate. By checking the first Dialog Memory option (the default), StatTools remembers the choices you make for any particular statistical analysis, so that it can make these same choices the next time you run the procedure. This saves you from having to start from scratch each time you run a regression or perform a time series analysis, say. I strongly recommend that you accept this default setting. The bottom dropdown list allows you to choose any of several slightly different methods for calculating percentiles. I suggest that you use the default method.

## Settings For Each Analysis

Besides choosing your favorite settings from the Application Settings dialog box, you can adjust these settings each time you run a statistical analysis. The dialog box for every statistical analysis, such as the one for one-variable summary statistics in Figure 2.35, has three buttons at the bottom left. The left button is for online help. The right button brings up the same Application Settings dialog box previously discussed.

*Figure 2.35*

*Typical*
*Dialog Box*

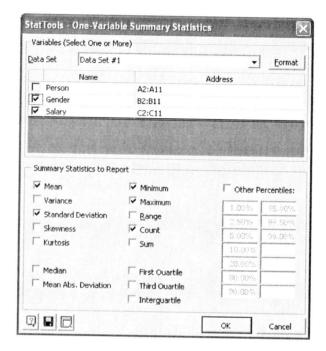

The middle button can be especially useful. It allows you to save the settings for this particular *procedure* and use them as the defaults for later uses. The one-variable procedure shown in Figure 2.35 is a good example of when this feature is useful. (I will discuss it in more detail in the next chapter.) The StatTools default is to check *all* of the summary statistics for the report. If you find that you typically want only a few, such as those checked here, you can click the middle button at the bottom, and you will be asked whether you want to save these settings. If you click on Yes, all future uses of the one variable summary statistics procedure will start with these summary statistics checked. This saves you from having to uncheck a lot of options you seldom need.

# 2.7 Getting Help

You shouldn't need too much help with StatTools, at least not after reading this book, but further help is available from several sources. First, you can find online help by selecting **StatTools Help** from the **Help** dropdown on the StatTools ribbon. This help system follows the same conventions as in most Windows help systems, as indicated in Figure 2.36.

*Figure 2.36*

*StatTools*
*Online Help*

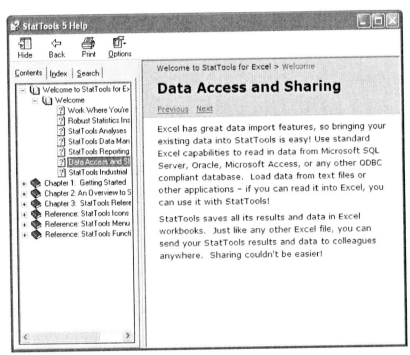

Second, you can read an online reference manual by selecting **Online Manual** from **Help** dropdown. This manual is written in Adobe Acrobat format, so it opens in Adobe Reader (or Adobe Acrobat, if you own it).

Third, you can click the **Help** icon in the dialog box for any analysis and get context sensitive help on that analysis.

Fourth, you can select **Getting Started Tutorial** from the **Help** dropdown for a web-based basic tutorial on StatTools.

Finally, by selecting **Example Spreadsheets** from the **Help** dropdown, you can view a number of worked-out examples, many very similar to those discussed in this book.

# Chapter 3: Summary Statistics

## 3.1 Introduction

**Summary Statistics Icon**

A good first step in analyzing a data set is to examine a few well-chosen summary measures and a few common graphs. In this chapter, I discuss numeric summary measures; in the next chapter, I discuss common graphs. The summary measures discussed here are of two types: those that summarize a single variable and those that measure the relationship between two variables.

## 3.2 One-Variable Summary Statistics

Suppose you have observations on a single numeric variable such as exam score. This variable contains the score on an exam for each student in a large university course. There are many numeric summary measures available to help you understand the distribution of scores, including the following:

- **Count** – number of scores

- **Sum** – sum of the scores

- **Mean** – average of the scores

- **Median** – score such that 50% are below it and 50% are above it

- **Mean absolute deviation** – average of absolute deviations from the mean

- **Standard deviation** and **variance** – measures of variability of scores

- **Minimum** and **maximum** – smallest and largest scores

- **First quartile** and **third quartile** – scores such that 25% are below and 25% are above

- **Interquartile range** – difference between third and first quartiles

- **Percentile** – score such that a given percentage are below it

- **Skewness** – measure of how far distribution is from being symmetric

- **Kurtosis** – measure of "thickness" of tails of distribution

StatTools can produce a table of any or all of these measures. These are illustrated with the data in Figure 3.1. (There are actually 212 observations, only a few of which are shown. The full data set is in the file **Exam Scores 1.xlsx**.) To obtain summary measures on the Score variable, select **One-Variable Summary** from the **Summary Statistics** dropdown to bring up the dialog box in Figure 3.2. You can check any or all of the options. If you check the **Other Percentiles** box, you can enter any percentiles you want. Note that for any percentile calculations (including the median and the quartiles), StatTools provides a number of percentile calculation methods, as selected from the Analyses group in the Application Settings dialog box. The method chosen typically won't make much difference in the results except for small or unusual data sets. I suggest that you use the default setting, **Automatic (Based on Input Data)**, for these calculations.

*Figure 3.1*

*Exam Score Data*

| Person | Score |
|--------|-------|
| 1 | 35 |
| 2 | 76 |
| 3 | 64 |
| 4 | 84 |
| 5 | 75 |
| 6 | 66 |
| 7 | 80 |
| 8 | 88 |
| 9 | 73 |
| 10 | 73 |

*Figure 3.2*

*One-Variable Summary Dialog Box*

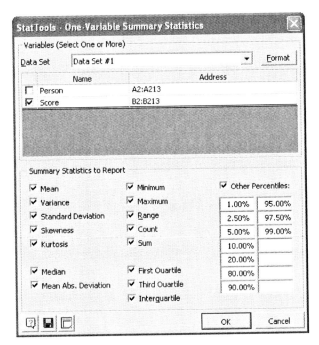

The output from these choices appears in Figure 3.3. It shows that there are 212 observations, which vary from a low of 24 to a high of 99. The average is about 67.5 and the standard deviation is about 18.0. The median score is 70, 25% of the scores are below 55, and 25% are above 82. The percentiles tell you, for example, that 2.5% of the scores are below 28 and 2.5% are above 95. Finally, as you might expect from exam scores, the data are negatively skewed, with a few low scores pulling down the mean.

**Figure 3.3**

*One-Variable Summary Output*

| One Variable Summary | Score Data Set #1 |
|---|---|
| Mean | 67.54 |
| Variance | 323.22 |
| Std. Dev. | 17.98 |
| Skewness | -0.4571 |
| Kurtosis | 2.4521 |
| Median | 70.00 |
| Mean Abs. Dev. | 14.88 |
| Minimum | 24.00 |
| Maximum | 99.00 |
| Range | 75.00 |
| Count | 212 |
| Sum | 14319.00 |
| 1st Quartile | 55.00 |
| 3rd Quartile | 82.00 |
| Interquartile Range | 27.00 |
| 1.00% | 26.00 |
| 2.50% | 28.00 |
| 5.00% | 33.00 |
| 10.00% | 42.00 |
| 20.00% | 52.00 |
| 80.00% | 84.00 |
| 90.00% | 89.00 |
| 95.00% | 94.00 |
| 97.50% | 95.00 |
| 99.00% | 97.00 |

## Summary Statistics for Stacked Data with a Categorical Variable

If one of the variables in the data set is categorical, such as gender, and the data are in stacked form, as in Figure 3.4 (see the file **Exam Scores 2.xlsx**), you can obtain summary measures for each category separately. To do this, select **One-Variable Summary** from the **Summary Statistics** dropdown, but in the resulting dialog box, select the **Stacked** format option and check the category and value boxes as in Figure 3.5. The output, shown in Figure 3.6, provides summary measures for each gender separately.

*Figure 3.4*

*Data in Stacked Form with Gender Variable*

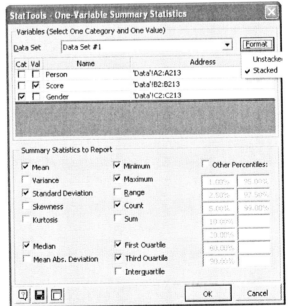

*Figure 3.5*

*One-Variable Summary Dialog Box for Stacked Data*

*Figure 3.6*

*Summary
Output for
Each
Gender*

| One Variable Summary | Score (Female) Data Set #1 | Score (Male) Data Set #1 |
|---|---|---|
| Mean | 68.21 | 66.98 |
| Std. Dev. | 16.94 | 18.87 |
| Median | 71.00 | 70.00 |
| Minimum | 24.00 | 24.00 |
| Maximum | 98.00 | 99.00 |
| Count | 97 | 115 |
| 1st Quartile | 58.00 | 54.00 |
| 3rd Quartile | 80.00 | 83.00 |

## Summary Statistics for Multiple Data Sets

In Chapter 2, I discussed the possibility of having multiple data sets in the same workbook. Most of the StatTools procedures allow you to work on multiple data sets simultaneously. There are certainly situations, depending on the procedure and the data sets, where this makes no sense, and you have to use common sense to recognize these situations. However, I will now illustrate a couple of situations where it makes perfect sense to obtain one-variable summary statistics for multiple data sets.

Consider the data in Figure 3.7. (See the file **Multiple Data Sets 1.xlsx**.) I defined the data in columns A–C as Data Set #1 and the data in columns E–F as Data Set #2. The fact that there are 10 people in each data set suggests that they are the *same* 10 people, in which case columns D and E could be deleted and a *single* combined data set could be defined. Nevertheless, I will keep the data sets separate for illustration.

*Figure 3.7*

*Multiple
Data Sets*

| Person | Gender | Salary | | Person | Age |
|---|---|---|---|---|---|
| 1 | Female | 47000 | | 1 | 30 |
| 2 | Male | 57700 | | 2 | 56 |
| 3 | Female | 72500 | | 3 | 43 |
| 4 | Female | 40700 | | 4 | 53 |
| 5 | Male | 91800 | | 5 | 33 |
| 6 | Male | 28500 | | 6 | 45 |
| 7 | Female | 52800 | | 7 | 56 |
| 8 | Male | 44000 | | 8 | 53 |
| 9 | Male | 42000 | | 9 | 47 |
| 10 | Female | 36200 | | 10 | 35 |

To obtain summary statistics on Salary and Age, fill in the One-Variable Summary Statistics dialog box as in Figure 3.8, selecting **All Data Sets** from the top dropdown list and checking any desired variables from each data set. The resulting output appears in Figure 3.9. Note that this procedure would work and make perfect sense even if the two groups of 10 people were different people. In this case, there could even be different numbers of people in the two data sets.

Figure 3.8

Dialog Box
with
Multiple
Data Sets

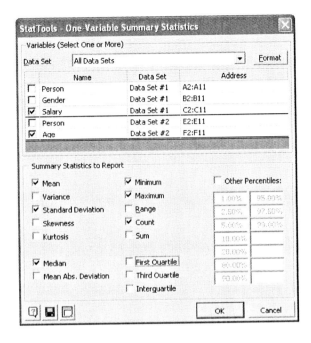

Figure 3.9

One-
Variable
Summary
Statistics
Output

| One Variable Summary | Salary<br>Data Set #1 | Age<br>Data Set #2 |
|---|---|---|
| Mean | 51320.00 | 45.100 |
| Std. Dev. | 18712.37 | 9.701 |
| Median | 44000.00 | 45.000 |
| Minimum | 28500.00 | 30.000 |
| Maximum | 91800.00 | 56.000 |
| Count | 10 | 10 |

A more interesting possibility is the following. Suppose a company has information on employees at each of three plants. The data for each plant is stored in a separate worksheet in a single workbook. For example, the data in Figure 3.10 are for the first few employees at plant 1. (See the file **Multiple Data Sets 2.xlsx** for the full data set. There are three worksheets, one for each of the plants, all set up like the one shown here, but they have different numbers of employees.) We defined a data set for each plant and gave them the descriptive names Plant1, Plant2, and Plant3.

Figure 3.10

One of
Several
Data Sets

| Employee | YrsExper | Salary |
|---|---|---|
| 1 | 5 | 41800 |
| 2 | 7 | 48600 |
| 3 | 4 | 41400 |
| 4 | 19 | 65800 |
| 5 | 10 | 47300 |
| 6 | 18 | 68900 |
| 7 | 1 | 22600 |
| 8 | 3 | 39600 |
| 9 | 14 | 61700 |

To obtain summary data for YrsExper and Salary for each of the 3 plants separately, fill in the One-Variable Summary Statistics dialog box as in Figure 3.11, selecting **All Data Sets** and checking the YrsExper and Salary variables for each of the data sets. The resulting output appears in Figure 3.12. Note how the column headings list the variable names and the data set names. This means that it is a good idea in this situation to give the data sets descriptive names rather than the StatTools default names.

Figure 3.11

*Dialog Box
with
Multiple
Data Sets*

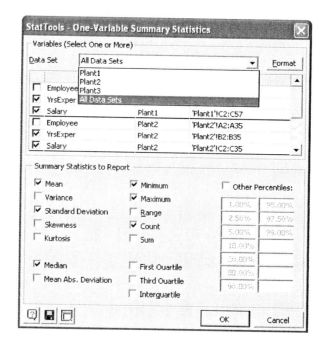

**Figure 3.12**

**One-Variable Summary Statistics Output**

| One Variable Summary | YrsExper Plant1 | Salary Plant1 | YrsExper Plant2 | Salary Plant2 | YrsExper Plant3 | Salary Plant3 |
|---|---|---|---|---|---|---|
| Mean | 9.982 | 49630.36 | 10.353 | 49911.76 | 9.529 | 49360.78 |
| Std. Dev. | 6.719 | 13769.09 | 5.175 | 11598.17 | 5.416 | 11065.03 |
| Median | 9.000 | 48100.00 | 10.000 | 49900.00 | 9.000 | 48200.00 |
| Minimum | 1.000 | 22600.00 | 1.000 | 27600.00 | 1.000 | 25800.00 |
| Maximum | 20.000 | 70600.00 | 20.000 | 70300.00 | 19.000 | 70400.00 |
| Count | 56 | 56 | 34 | 34 | 51 | 51 |

## Notes

- In this book I adopt the convention of formatting numerical results to 2 or 3 decimal places in most cases. However, you can specify the numeric format to be used in reports for each variable in the Data Set Manager. You do this through the Output Format column. This allows you to override StatTools's "auto" setting.

- You can simultaneously request summary measures for any number of numeric variables. For example, if this data set had exam scores for four different exams, each in a separate column, you could obtain summary measures for all four exams by checking the corresponding variables in the dialog box in Figure 3.2. Alternatively, if the data were in unstacked form, with separate columns for male scores and female scores, you could select both variables to get the type of output in Figure 3.6.

- If you consistently ask for only a few of the summary measures, such as the count, mean, standard deviation, and median, say, you can uncheck all boxes except these and then click on the middle button at the bottom left of the dialog box in Figure 3.2. This saves the settings as your "favorites." Of course, you can override these settings on any future run, but this feature saves you from unchecking a lot of unwanted options each time through.

# 3.3 Correlation and Covariance

The summary measures in the previous section summarize each selected variable separately. They tell you nothing about possible relationships between the variables. There are many ways to examine and measure relationships between variables. In this section, I discuss a relatively simple set of measures, **correlations** and **covariances**. Each of these measures the strength of a *linear* relationship between two variables. Correlations are more common and easier to understand, but covariances are also important in certain situations, such as portfolio analysis in finance.

A correlation between two variables is a unitless measure, always between −1 and +1. The closer its magnitude is to 1, either negative or positive, the stronger the *linear* relationship is between these two variables. If the correlation is close to 0, there is virtually no linear relationship, although in some rare cases there can still be a *nonlinear* relationship. A covariance between two variables is the correlation multiplied by the product of the two standard deviations. It is strongly affected by the units of measurement, so its absolute magnitude is difficult to interpret. For example, a covariance between two variables could be 3 or 3000, depending on whether one of the variables is measured in dollars or thousands of dollars.

When there are several potentially related numeric variables, it is common to request a table of correlations and/or a table of covariances. Each entry in either table is the correlation or covariance between the row and column variables, with 1's on the diagonal (for correlations) or variances on the diagonal (for covariances). These tables are symmetric—entries below the diagonal are a mirror image of those above the diagonal—so it makes sense to request entries only above (or below) the diagonal. StatTools gives you this option.

These measures are illustrated with the stock return data shown in Figure 3.13. These are monthly returns for a 46-month period for American Express, Federal Express, General Motors, IBM, McDonald's, and Microsoft. (The full data set is in the file **Stock Returns.xlsx**.) To obtain correlations and/or covariances for these six variables, select **Correlation and Covariance** from the **Summary Statistics** dropdown and fill in the resulting dialog box as in Figure 3.14. Here, I checked the variable for each company, requested both a table of correlations and a table of covariances, and asked only for entries on and above the diagonal.

*Figure 3.13*

*Monthly
Stock
Return Data*

| Date | AXP | FDX | GM | IBM | MCD | MSFT |
|------|-----|-----|-----|-----|-----|------|
| 01-Mar-96 | 0.076 | -0.055 | 0.039 | -0.093 | -0.040 | 0.044 |
| 01-Apr-96 | -0.013 | 0.155 | 0.019 | -0.031 | -0.003 | 0.100 |
| 01-May-96 | -0.056 | -0.051 | 0.024 | -0.009 | 0.005 | 0.048 |
| 01-Jun-96 | -0.025 | 0.070 | -0.050 | -0.073 | -0.029 | 0.011 |
| 01-Jul-96 | -0.015 | -0.051 | -0.069 | 0.086 | -0.008 | -0.019 |
| 01-Aug-96 | 0.000 | -0.037 | 0.026 | 0.064 | 0.000 | 0.040 |
| 01-Sep-96 | 0.057 | 0.059 | -0.033 | 0.088 | 0.021 | 0.077 |
| 01-Oct-96 | 0.021 | 0.016 | 0.117 | 0.036 | -0.060 | 0.040 |
| 01-Nov-96 | 0.111 | 0.099 | 0.082 | 0.235 | 0.050 | 0.143 |
| 01-Dec-96 | 0.086 | 0.006 | -0.033 | -0.049 | -0.030 | 0.053 |

*Figure 3.14*

*Dialog Box
for
Correlations,
Covariances*

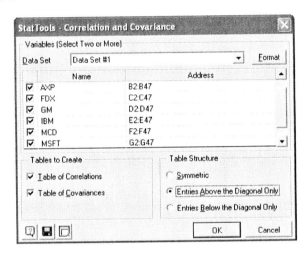

The output appears in Figure 3.15. All of the stock return variables are positively correlated, but none of the correlations is very large, the largest being the 0.483 correlation between American Express and General Motors. The covariances provide essentially the same information, but because they are scaled by the standard deviations of returns (small numbers), they are more difficult to interpret. (Nevertheless, these covariances are used directly in a commonly applied risk–return portfolio selection model in finance.)

**Figure 3.15**

**Tables of Correlations and Covariances**

| Correlation Table | AXP Data Set #1 | FDX Data Set #1 | GM Data Set #1 | IBM Data Set #1 | MCD Data Set #1 | MSFT Data Set #1 |
|---|---|---|---|---|---|---|
| AXP | 1.000 | 0.400 | 0.483 | 0.358 | 0.354 | 0.361 |
| FDX | | 1.000 | 0.250 | 0.292 | 0.265 | 0.119 |
| GM | | | 1.000 | 0.259 | 0.318 | 0.303 |
| IBM | | | | 1.000 | 0.397 | 0.313 |
| MCD | | | | | 1.000 | 0.289 |
| MSFT | | | | | | 1.000 |

| Covariance Table | AXP Data Set #1 | FDX Data Set #1 | GM Data Set #1 | IBM Data Set #1 | MCD Data Set #1 | MSFT Data Set #1 |
|---|---|---|---|---|---|---|
| AXP | 0.00658 | 0.00369 | 0.00319 | 0.00270 | 0.00205 | 0.00325 |
| FDX | | 0.01295 | 0.00231 | 0.00309 | 0.00216 | 0.00151 |
| GM | | | 0.00661 | 0.00196 | 0.00185 | 0.00273 |
| IBM | | | | 0.00866 | 0.00264 | 0.00323 |
| MCD | | | | | 0.00512 | 0.00229 |
| MSFT | | | | | | 0.01229 |

3.3 Correlation and Covariance

# Chapter 4: Summary Graphs

## 4.1 Introduction

**Summary Graphs Icon**

Numeric summary measures of a data set are great, but they typically cannot convey as much information as well-chosen graphs. At the very least, the graphs discussed in this chapter are a welcome addition to tables of numbers. Statisticians have devised a great many types of graphs for summarizing data, all with the goal of adding insights. StatTools implements the most common of these, including the three types discussed in this chapter: histograms, scatterplots, and box-whisker plots. These three are "general-purpose" graphs. More specialized graphs appear in later chapters.

## 4.2 Histograms

A **histogram** is essentially a bar chart that shows how the data for a single variable are distributed. We divide the range for the variable into a number of categories, typically called **bins**, count the number of observations in each bin, and graph these counts. The only difficult part of this procedure, from a user's standpoint, is choosing the bins. This choice can have a significant impact on the shape of the resulting histogram—and the information it conveys. If there are two few bins, you don't see a real distribution of the data, whereas if there are too many bins, the histogram looks too "noisy." It takes some thought and experimentation to find appropriate bins, and there is usually not a single correct choice. Fortunately, StatTools chooses a default set of bins for you, based on the number of observations and the range of the data. You can override this choice if you like, but it is often perfectly adequate.

The StatTools histogram procedure is illustrated with the exam score data from the previous chapter. (See the file **Exam Scores 2.xlsx**.) Recall that this file contains the score on an exam for each of 212 students, where each student is identified as a male or a female. The scores vary from a low of 24 to a high of 99. A portion of the data is repeated in Figure 4.1. To obtain a histogram of these scores for both genders combined, select **Histogram** from the **Summary Graphs** dropdown. In the resulting dialog box, shown in Figure 4.2, select the Score variable and accept all default settings in the bottom section. In particular, allow StatTools to choose the bins, and choose to plot Frequency (the counts) on the Y-axis.

*Figure 4.1*

**Exam Score Data**

| Person | Score | Gender |
|---|---|---|
| 1 | 35 | Female |
| 2 | 76 | Male |
| 3 | 64 | Male |
| 4 | 84 | Male |
| 5 | 75 | Female |
| 6 | 66 | Male |
| 7 | 80 | Male |
| 8 | 88 | Male |
| 9 | 73 | Male |

*Figure 4.2*

**Histogram Dialog Box with Default Settings**

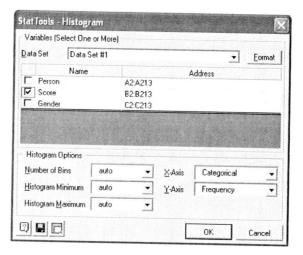

The resulting histogram appears in Figure 4.3. StatTools first calculates the data shown in Figure 4.4 and then creates the histogram from this data. Note that it has chosen 9 bins, the first extending from 24.00 to 32.33 with midpoint 28.17, and so on. The midpoints of the bins are used to label the horizontal axis. This histogram certainly provides a good visual impression of the exam score distribution. There is some skewness to the left, and the highest bars indicate the most frequent score ranges.

Figure 4.3

Histogram
with Default
Bins

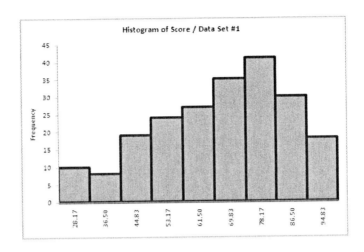

Figure 4.4

Data for
Histogram

| Histogram | Bin Min | Bin Max | Bin Midpoint | Freq. | Rel. Freq. | Prb. Density |
|---|---|---|---|---|---|---|
| | | | Score / Data Set #1 | | | |
| Bin #1 | 24.00 | 32.33 | 28.17 | 10 | 0.0472 | 0.006 |
| Bin #2 | 32.33 | 40.67 | 36.50 | 8 | 0.0377 | 0.005 |
| Bin #3 | 40.67 | 49.00 | 44.83 | 19 | 0.0896 | 0.011 |
| Bin #4 | 49.00 | 57.33 | 53.17 | 24 | 0.1132 | 0.014 |
| Bin #5 | 57.33 | 65.67 | 61.50 | 27 | 0.1274 | 0.015 |
| Bin #6 | 65.67 | 74.00 | 69.83 | 35 | 0.1651 | 0.020 |
| Bin #7 | 74.00 | 82.33 | 78.17 | 41 | 0.1934 | 0.023 |
| Bin #8 | 82.33 | 90.67 | 86.50 | 30 | 0.1415 | 0.017 |
| Bin #9 | 90.67 | 99.00 | 94.83 | 18 | 0.0849 | 0.010 |

The bins chosen automatically by StatTools do not typically have "nice" endpoints. The dialog box in Figure 4.5 indicates how you can override the default settings with your own customized settings. Because the scores range from the 20s to the 90s, it is natural to have 8 equal-width bins, starting at 20 and ending at 100. The first bin goes from 20 to 30, the second from 30 to 40, and so on. With these "nice" bins, the resulting histogram appears in Figure 4.6. It conveys about the same information as the default histogram, but it would probably be preferred for aesthetic reasons by most people. Note that we also elected to display relative frequencies on the Y-axis in this histogram. (A relative frequency is the fraction of observations in a given category.) This choice simply scales the heights of the bars, but it makes no difference to the overall shape. You could also choose to display probability density values on the Y-axis (so that the area under the histogram is 1), but these too just scale the heights; they have no effect on the shape.

*Figure 4.5*

**Histogram
Dialog Box
with
Customized
Settings**

*Figure 4.6*

**Histogram
with
Customized
Bins**

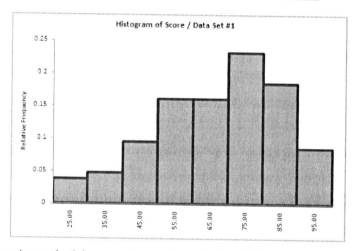

If the data are in stacked form, with a categorical variable such as Gender, then you can get a separate histogram for each category. To do so, fill in the histogram dialog box as in Figure 4.7, selecting the Stacked format and checking the categorical and value variables. You then get two histograms. The one for females appears in Figure 4.8. The one for males (not shown) is similar. This allows for an easy comparison of the female and male score distributions.

---

**4.2 Histograms**

*Figure 4.7*

**Histogram
Dialog Box
with
Stacked
Data**

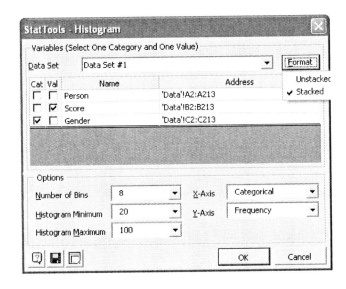

*Figure 4.8*

**Histogram
of Female
Scores**

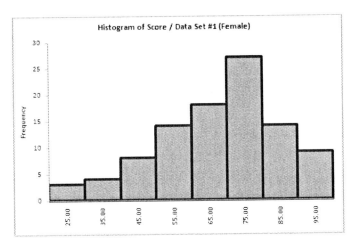

## Notes

- StatTools allows you to simultaneously request histograms for any number of numeric variables. For example, if this data set had exam scores for four different exams, each in a separate column, you could obtain a separate histogram for each exam by checking the corresponding variables in the histogram dialog box. Alternatively, if the data were in unstacked form, with separate columns for male scores and female scores, you could select both variables to get the type of output in Figure 4.8

- Technically, each bin includes its right endpoint but not its left endpoint. So, for example, the bin from 30 to 40 includes all values greater than 30 and less than or equal to 40.

- A variable that is virtually unlimited in one or both directions is problematic for any histogram, including those produced by StatTools. For example, suppose your data set includes a salary variable, with the vast majority of salaries under $100,000, but with a few salaries up in the millions. If you want the histogram to include these large salaries, then they will essentially dominate the histogram, with virtually all of the "normal" salaries in one or two bars to the left. The only alternative is to specify your own Histogram Maximum, such as $150,000. Then the histogram will simply ignore the really large salaries and show the shape of the distribution of the "normal" salaries much more clearly.

# 4.3 Scatterplots

A **scatterplot** illustrates the relationship between two numeric variables. It is customary to denote one of the variables as the Y variable (for the vertical axis) and the other as the X variable (for the horizontal axis). Then each observation on the two variables corresponds to a point with coordinates (X,Y). You can then examine the shape of the resulting scatter of points for patterns, such as an upward or downward trend, a linear relationship, or a nonlinear relationship.

To illustrate scatterplots, consider the data in Figure 4.9. (This shows only the first few observations. The full data set is in the file **Expenses.xlsx**.) Each observation shows the annual salary for a family and how much that family spends annually on cultural events, sports, and dining out. A table of correlations between these variables, as discussed in the previous chapter, appears in Figure 4.10. In particular, the top row shows how each of the spending variables correlates with salary. Clearly, families who earn higher salaries tend to spend more on cultural events and dining out. However, no such relationship appears between salary and sports.

*Figure 4.9*

*Expense Data*

| Salary | Culture | Sports | Dining |
|--------|---------|--------|--------|
| $54,600 | $1,020 | $990 | $1,510 |
| $57,500 | $1,100 | $460 | $1,180 |
| $53,300 | $900 | $780 | $1,590 |
| $43,500 | $570 | $860 | $1,750 |
| $57,200 | $900 | $1,390 | $2,120 |
| $63,400 | $820 | $1,880 | $3,090 |
| $58,500 | $1,340 | $710 | $1,540 |
| $55,600 | $1,250 | $680 | $1,800 |
| $61,300 | $1,190 | $1,220 | $2,330 |

*Figure 4.10*

*Correlations for Expense Data*

| Correlation Table | Salary Data Set #1 | Culture Data Set #1 | Sports Data Set #1 | Dining Data Set #1 |
|-------------------|--------------------|---------------------|--------------------|--------------------|
| Salary | 1.000 | 0.506 | -0.081 | 0.558 |
| Culture | | 1.000 | -0.520 | 0.170 |
| Sports | | | 1.000 | 0.266 |
| Dining | | | | 1.000 |

You can see these relationships, or lack of them, better with scatterplots. To create scatterplots between Salary and each of the other variables, select **Scatterplots** from the **Summary Graphs** dropdown and fill in the resulting dialog box as in Figure 4.11. Note that each variable you check can play the role of an X variable or a Y variable, but not both. Once you select the variables, StatTools creates a scatterplot of each selected Y versus each selected X. (In the example shown, there will be a scatterplot of Salary versus each of the spending variables.) You can also check the **Display Correlation Coefficient** option to have the corresponding correlation displayed next to the scatterplot.

**Figure 4.11**

**Scatterplot
Dialog Box**

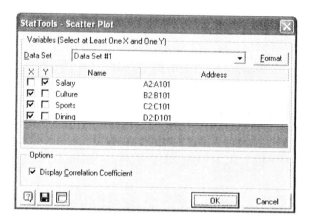

Two of the three requested scatterplots appear in Figure 4.12 and Figure 4.13. The first, of Salary versus Culture, suggests an upward sloping linear relationship between the two variables. However, if you imagine a straight line fit through these points, there is far from a perfect fit. This is essentially what a correlation of 0.506 means: a linear relationship, but far from a perfect one. In contrast, the scatterplot of Salary versus Sports indicates no linear relationship, just a swarm of points. This is not surprising, given the negligible correlation of –0.081.

**Figure 4.12**

**Scatterplot
of Salary
Versus
Culture**

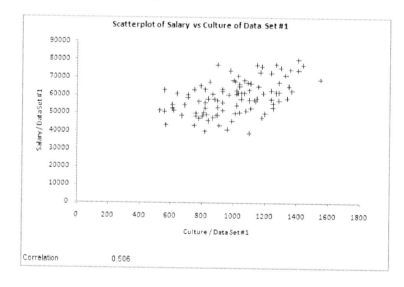

*Figure 4.13*

**Scatterplot of Salary Versus Sports**

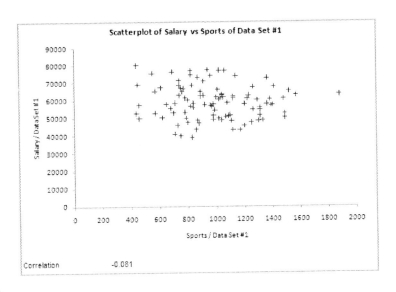

## Notes

- This example used the Culture, Sports, and Dining variables as X's. If you want to create scatterplots between any of these variables, such as Culture versus Dining, you have to use the scatterplot procedure a second time, designating one of these variables as Y.

# 4.4 Box-Whisker Plots

**Box-whisker plots** (or simply **boxplots**) provide an alternative to histograms for describing a distribution of data graphically. They are especially good for comparing two (or more) distributions, such as female exam scores versus male exam scores.

Boxplots are easiest to describe by means of an example, so I again use the exam score data in the file **Exam Scores 2.xlsx**. I first obtain a single box-whisker plot for all of the exam scores. To do this, select **Box-Whisker Plot** from the **Summary Graphs** dropdown and fill in the resulting dialog box as in Figure 4.14. By checking the **Include Key Describing Plot Elements** option, you obtain a guide to the meaning of box-whisker elements. This is for learning purposes only, and you probably won't ever check this option once you get used to boxplots.

*Figure 4.14*

*Dialog Box for Single Box-Whisker Plot*

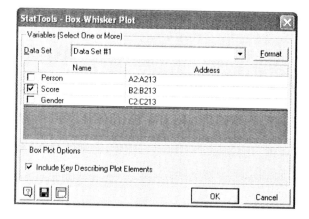

The resulting box-whisker plot appears in Figure 4.15. To interpret it, StatTools provides the key in Figure 4.16. This key indicates that the box extends from the first quartile to the third quartile, so that it contains the middle 50% of the data. The vertical line in the middle of the box is positioned at the median, and the red x inside the box is positioned at the mean. The lines extending from either side of the box—the "whiskers"—extend almost to the extremes of the data, as explained in the key. However, mild and extreme outliers are marked separately. As is apparent from this plot of exam scores, there is a slight skewness to the left (because the left whisker is longer than the right one and the mean is to the left of the median), and there are no outliers.

---

**Figure 4.15**

*Box-*
*Whisker*
*Plot of All*
*Exam*
*Scores*

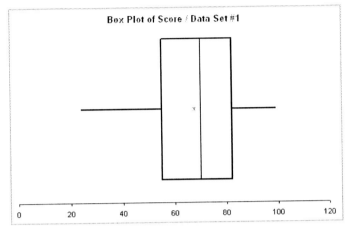

**Figure 4.16**

*Key to*
*Elements of*
*Box-*
*Whisker*
*Plot*

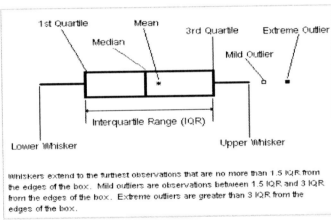

In a data set such as this one, with a gender categorical variable and the data in stacked format, it is useful to create side-by-side box-whisker plots, one for females and one for males. To do so, fill in the box-whisker dialog box as in Figure 4.17, making sure to select the stacked format option and choose the categorical and value variables. (This time, it is not necessary to request a key; it is always the same.) The resulting box-whisker plots appear in Figure 4.18. These plots indicate that the distributions for females and males are quite similar, although there is one outlier for the females.

*Figure 4.17*

*Dialog Box for Side-by-Side Box-Whisker Plots*

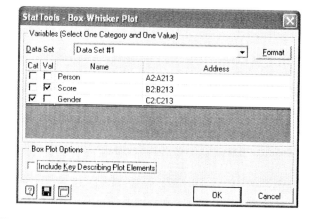

*Figure 4.18*

*Side-by-Side Box-Whisker Plots for Females and Males*

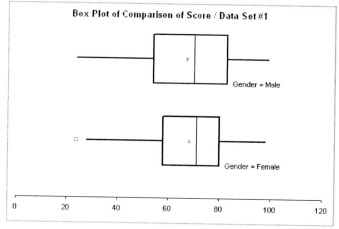

## Notes

- The key shown in Figure 2.16 is always the same—that is, it doesn't depend on the particular data set, and it is not drawn to scale accurately. Its only purpose is to remind you of the various elements of a boxplot.

# Chapter 5: Statistical Inference

## 5.1 Introduction

*Statistical Inference Icon*

In the previous two chapters, I discussed tabular and graphical procedures for summarizing the observed data. I now take the point of view that the observed data set is really a random sample from some larger population of data, and your objective is to infer properties of the population from the sample data. In this chapter, I discuss the two general methods for making inferences: confidence intervals and hypothesis tests. Statisticians have devised confidence intervals and hypothesis tests for an almost unlimited variety of situations. StatTools implements the most common of these.

## 5.2 Confidence Intervals

Suppose there is a population parameter, such as a mean or the difference between means, that you want to infer. You observe the sample data and use it to calculate an interval based on a selected confidence level, usually 95%. The meaning of the resulting interval, called a **95% confidence level**, is that you are 95% sure that the population parameter is within this interval. The 95% confidence level is the most common. However, it is just as easy to use a 90% or 99% confidence level, two levels that are also frequently chosen, and StatTools allows you to choose whatever confidence level you want.

### Confidence Interval for a Mean or Standard Deviation[1]

Two common measures of a distribution are its mean and standard deviation. The first is a measure of central tendency, whereas the second is a measure of variability. You might be interested in inferring either or both of these, based on a random sample from a population. StatTools allows you to obtain a confidence interval for each.

Suppose you are interested in the distribution of regular unleaded gasoline prices across the country at a particular point in time. You randomly select 32 gas stations and record the per gallon prices. Several of these appear in Figure 5.1. (See the file **Gas Prices.xlsx** for the full data set. By the way, as I am writing this chapter, gas prices are under $2, but by the time you read this, they could easily be as high as those in the example, or even higher!)

---

[1] In StatTools 5.0 and earlier, the menu item for these analyses was simply **Confidence Interval**. With the addition of confidence intervals for proportions in version 5.5, the menu item has been renamed to **Confidence Interval for Mean/Std. Deviation**.

Figure 5.1

Gasoline
Prices

| Gas station | Price of regular unleaded |
|---|---|
| 1 | 3.19 |
| 2 | 3.30 |
| 3 | 3.24 |
| 4 | 3.34 |
| 5 | 3.29 |
| 6 | 3.25 |
| 7 | 3.32 |
| 8 | 3.38 |
| 9 | 3.28 |
| 10 | 3.28 |

To get some idea of the distribution of these prices within the sample, the one-variable summary procedure (as explained in Chapter 3) is useful. See the output in Figure 5.2. This indicates that the mean and standard deviation of prices *in the sample* are $3.279 and $0.079. But what about the population as a whole?

Figure 5.2

Summary
Measures
of Gasoline
Prices

| One Variable Summary | Price of regular unleaded Data Set #1 |
|---|---|
| Mean | 3.279 |
| Std. Dev. | 0.079 |
| Minimum | 3.140 |
| Maximum | 3.460 |
| Count | 32 |

You can never know the population mean and standard deviation (without taking a census of *all* gas stations), but you can obtain confidence intervals for these parameters. This is called a **one-sample** procedure, which means that we are interested in only a *single* population of all gas stations (as opposed, say, to comparing those in the East with those in the West). To perform the analysis, select **Confidence Interval for Mean/Std. Deviation** from the **Statistical Inference** dropdown and fill in the resulting dialog box as shown in Figure 5.3, making sure to select **One-Sample Analysis** from the top dropdown list. (Note: A few of the screenshots in this chapter are from an advanced copy of StatTools 5.5. This version includes new confidence interval and hypothesis test analyses involving proportions; hence, the distinguishing title in Figure 5.3. Also, the three bottom buttons have a slightly different look.) The resulting output appears in Figure 5.4. The 95% confidence interval for the mean extends from $3.250 to $3.308, and the 95% confidence interval for the standard deviation extends from $0.064 to $0.106.

**Figure 5.3**

**Confidence Interval Dialog Box for One-Sample Procedure**

**Figure 5.4**

**Confidence Intervals for Mean and Standard Deviation**

| Conf. Intervals (One-Sample) | Price of regular unleaded Data Set #1 |
|---|---|
| Sample Size | 32 |
| Sample Mean | 3.279 |
| Sample Std Dev | 0.079 |
| Confidence Level (Mean) | 95.0% |
| Degrees of Freedom | 31 |
| Lower Limit | 3.250 |
| Upper Limit | 3.308 |
| Confidence Level (Std Dev) | 95.0% |
| Degrees of Freedom | 31 |
| Lower Limit | 0.064 |
| Upper Limit | 0.106 |

### Notes

- The formulas for these confidence intervals are "live." In particular, you can change either of the confidence levels in Figure 5.4, and the confidence limits will change automatically. For example, you can get a tighter confidence interval by using a lower confidence level. When the confidence level for the mean is set to 90%, the confidence interval then extends from $3.255 to $3.303.

- The confidence interval for the mean is always centered at the sample mean, in this case $3.279. This is not the case for the confidence interval for the standard deviation. The sample standard deviation is always closer to the *left* endpoint of the confidence interval.

## Confidence Interval for a Difference Between Means

A common problem in statistics is to compare two populations on some attribute. For example, assume that a number of customers have been asked to rate their satisfaction with a restaurant's new sandwich on a scale of 1 to 10. Each customer is identified as a male or a female. On average, how well do the customers like this sandwich? Does the answer depend on gender? One way to answer these questions is to construct confidence intervals for the mean rating. This can actually be done in two ways. You can construct two separate confidence intervals, one for males and one for females, and then compare them visually. Alternatively (and preferably), you can construct a single confidence for the mean *difference* in ratings between males and females.

The data for this example are in stacked format, as shown in Figure 5.5. (There are actually 110 customers total. See the file **Sandwich Ratings.xlsx** for the full data set.) There is a "Category" column that identifies gender, and there is a "Value" column that identifies the customers' satisfaction ratings.

*Figure 5.5*

*Satisfaction Ratings in Stacked Form*

| Customer | Gender | Satisfaction |
|---|---|---|
| 1 | Male | 9 |
| 2 | Male | 8 |
| 3 | Male | 6 |
| 4 | Male | 8 |
| 5 | Female | 7 |
| 6 | Female | 6 |
| 7 | Female | 7 |
| 8 | Male | 9 |
| 9 | Male | 7 |
| 10 | Male | 7 |
| 11 | Male | 6 |
| 12 | Male | 10 |
| 13 | Female | 2 |
| 14 | Male | 7 |
| 15 | Male | 8 |

Before requesting confidence intervals, it is always a good idea to get a better understanding of the data by requesting summary measures or comparison charts. I first asked for a few summary measures, grouped by gender, as explained in Chapter 3. This produces the output in Figure 5.6. Apparently, the males tend to rate the sandwich higher than the females. A similar comparison can be done graphically with box-whisker plots, as explained in Chapter 4. The resulting graph appears in Figure 5.7. It confirms that the male ratings tend to be higher than the female ratings, although there is considerable variability in each group's ratings.

*Figure 5.61*

*One-
Variable
Summary
Output*

| One Variable Summary | Satisfaction (Female) Data Set #1 | Satisfaction (Male) Data Set #1 |
|---|---|---|
| Mean | 5.949 | 6.746 |
| Std. Dev. | 2.470 | 1.787 |
| Minimum | 1.000 | 2.000 |
| Maximum | 10.000 | 10.000 |
| Count | 39 | 71 |

*Figure 5.72*

*Box-
Whisker
Plot*

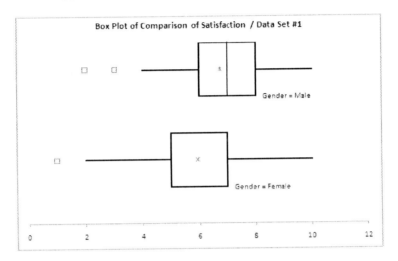

We now look at confidence intervals. To obtain a confidence interval for the mean rating for each group separately, select **Confidence Interval for Mean/Std. Deviation** from the **Statistical Inference** dropdown and fill in the dialog box as in Figure 5.8. Note that the One-Sample Analysis option has been chosen. This means that each gender's ratings are treated separately. The resulting output appears in Figure 5.9. A 95% confidence for the mean rating of all females extends from 5.148 to 6.750. This is based on the 39 females in the sample. In contrast, a 95% confidence interval for the mean rating of all males extends from 6.324 to 7.169, which is based on the 71 males in the sample. Clearly, the male confidence interval is a bit to the right of the female confidence interval, although they overlap considerably.

Figure 5.8

**Confidence Interval Dialog Box for One-Sample Analysis**

**StatTools - Confidence Interval for Mean/Std. Deviation**

Analysis Type: One-Sample Analysis

Variables (Select One Category and One Value)

Data Set: Data Set #1 | Format

| Cat | Val | Name | Address |
|-----|-----|------|---------|
| ☐ | ☐ | Customer | A2:A111 |
| ☑ | ☐ | Gender | B2:B111 |
| ☐ | ☑ | Satisfaction | C2:C111 |

Confidence Intervals to Calculate

☑ For the Mean          Confidence Level  95%

☐ For the Standard Deviation      Confidence Level  95%

OK    Cancel

**Figure 5.9**

**Confidence Interval Output for One-Sample Analysis**

| Conf. Intervals (One-Sample) | Satisfaction (Female) Data Set #1 | Satisfaction (Male) Data Set #1 |
|---|---|---|
| Sample Size | 39 | 71 |
| Sample Mean | 5.949 | 6.746 |
| Sample Std Dev | 2.470 | 1.787 |
| Confidence Level (Mean) | 95.0% | 95.0% |
| Degrees of Freedom | 38 | 70 |
| Lower Limit | 5.148 | 6.324 |
| Upper Limit | 6.750 | 7.169 |

A more appropriate procedure is to find a confidence interval for the *difference* between male and female ratings. This requires a **two-sample** procedure. To perform the analysis, select **Confidence Interval** from the **Statistical Inference** dropdown, but now fill out the dialog box as in Figure 5.10, making sure to select the Two-Sample Analysis option.

**Figure 5.10**

**Confidence
Interval
Dialog Box
for Two-
Sample
Analysis**

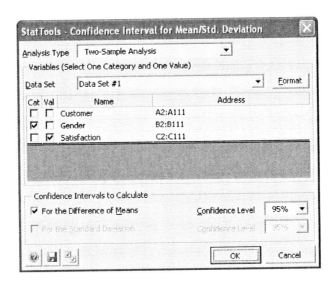

The resulting output appears in Figure 5.11. Note that there are two columns in the middle section, one for equal variances and one for unequal variances. The correct procedure depends on whether the variance of ratings is the *same* for males as for females. Based on the sample standard deviations, 2.470 for females and 1.787 for males, there is a fairly large difference between the two variances. Therefore, the "Unequal Variances" column for the confidence intervals is more appropriate, although the difference is slight. (This is confirmed by the bottom section, which is a formal test of equality of variances. A small p-value in this test—less than 0.05, say—is convincing evidence of *unequal* variances.)

**Figure 5.11**

**Confidence
Interval
Output for
Two-
Sample
Analysis**

| Sample Summaries | Satisfaction (Female) Data Set #1 | Satisfaction (Male) Data Set #1 |
|---|---|---|
| Sample Size | 39 | 71 |
| Sample Mean | 5.949 | 6.746 |
| Sample Std Dev | 2.470 | 1.787 |

| Conf. Intervals (Difference of Means) | Equal Variances | Unequal Variances |
|---|---|---|
| Confidence Level | 95.0% | 95.0% |
| Sample Mean Difference | -0.798 | -0.798 |
| Standard Error of Difference | 0.409 | 0.449 |
| Degrees of Freedom | 108 | 60 |
| Lower Limit | -1.609 | -1.696 |
| Upper Limit | 0.013 | 0.100 |

| Equality of Variances Test | |
|---|---|
| Ratio of Sample Variances | 1.9119 |
| p-Value | 0.0190 |

The confidence interval in the "Unequal Variances" column extends from −1.696 to 0.100. Because this is a confidence interval for the mean female rating minus the mean male rating, it provides evidence that the mean female rating is smaller—perhaps as much as 1.696 smaller. On the other hand, because the upper limit of this interval is a positive number, 0.100, there is still some chance that the mean female rating is *larger*.

**Notes**

- This same analysis could be accomplished with data in unstacked form. In this case the data would have to be set up so that there are two columns, one for the 39 female ratings and one for the 71 male ratings. There would no longer be a single long "Satisfaction" column, and there would be no need for the Gender column. Given this setup, the same StatTools procedures could be used, with obvious changes in the dialog boxes, to obtain exactly the same results.

- Why is the difference in Figure 5.11 shown as Female minus Male, not the opposite? For stacked data, StatTools's convention is to make the first variable in the difference correspond to the category that comes first in alphabetical order. However, you will notice when you run this two-sample procedure that another dialog box (not shown here) asks you whether you want to analyze in reverse order. If you check this option, then the confidence interval will be for the mean of males minus the mean of females.

## Confidence Interval with Paired Samples

Sometimes you want to compare two means, but the two samples you observe are paired in an obvious way. In this case, the two-sample test discussed in the previous section is not appropriate. Instead, it is appropriate to use a **paired-sample** procedure. This is essentially a one-sample procedure on the *differences* between the observations in each pair.

As an example, consider the data in Figure 5.12. (There are actually 28 rows of data. See the file **Before-After Tests.xlsx** for the full data set.) In this example, 28 people take a course in some technical skill. Before the course begins, they take a test in the skill, with the results in column B. After the course, they take a similar test, with the results in column C. This is a situation where a paired-sample procedure is clearly appropriate. The reason is that the observations in columns B and C tend to be correlated. People who score relatively low (or high) on the first test tend to score relatively low (or high) on the second test. (In fact, the correlation between the two sets of scores is quite high, 0.729.)

Figure 5.3

Paired
Observations

| Person | ScoreBefore | ScoreAfter |
|--------|-------------|------------|
| 1 | 50 | 86 |
| 2 | 50 | 81 |
| 3 | 56 | 76 |
| 4 | 49 | 82 |
| 5 | 41 | 68 |
| 6 | 49 | 73 |
| 7 | 40 | 74 |
| 8 | 38 | 72 |
| 9 | 39 | 70 |
| 10 | 23 | 62 |
| 11 | 47 | 78 |
| 12 | 15 | 60 |

Our interest here is probably not in the mean score of either test but rather in the mean difference — that is, *improvement* — from the first test to the second test. To create a confidence interval for this mean difference, select **Confidence Interval for Mean/Std. Deviation** from the **Statistical Inference** dropdown and fill out the resulting dialog box as in Figure 5.13. Note in particular the Analysis Type in the top dropdown list. To use this procedure, the data must be in unstacked form, with the two paired sets of observations in separate variables.

**Figure 5.13**

**Dialog Box
for Paired-
Sample
Procedure**

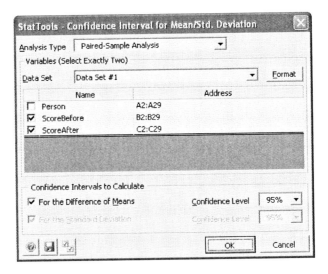

The results appear in Figure 5.14. (Again, there is another dialog box, not shown here, that allows you to reverse the differences. I did this, so that the differences analyzed are ScoreAfter minus ScoreBefore, that is, the improvement.) With this in mind, the mean improvement observed is 30.5, and a 95% confidence interval for the mean improvement extends from 27.946 to 33.054. The interpretation is that if a whole population of similar students took this course, along with the before and after tests, we are 95% confident that their average improvement would be inside this interval.

**Figure 5.14**

*Confidence
Interval for
Paired-
Sample
Procedure*

| Conf. Intervals (Paired-Sample) | ScoreAfter - ScoreBefore |
|---|---|
| Sample Size | 28 |
| Sample Mean | 30.5 |
| Sample Std Dev | 6.586 |
| Confidence Level | 95.0% |
| Degrees of Freedom | 27 |
| Lower Limit | 27.946 |
| Upper Limit | 33.054 |

### Notes

- It is possible to run the two-sample procedure on paired data, but the results will be misleading because of the correlation between pairs. In general, the two-sample confidence interval for the mean difference will be *wider* than the correct confidence interval from the paired procedure.

- Because the observations must be paired, there must be an equal number of observations in the two paired variables. This is not a requirement for the two-sample procedure from the previous section.

- Why did I need to *reverse* the difference to make them "ScoreBefore minus ScoreAfter," not the opposite? For data in unstacked form, StatTools's convention is to make the first variable in the difference correspond to the one that is to the *left* of the other in the worksheet.

## Confidence Interval for a Proportion[2]

One common set of analyses that has been missing from StatTools is statistical inference on proportions: a confidence interval for a proportion, a confidence interval for the difference between two proportions, and corresponding hypothesis tests. These analyses are finally available in version 5.5. (Note: The terms *proportion* and *percentage* are used interchangeably in this section. Each is a number between 0 and 1.)

A typical example occurs before elections, when we are bombarded by the results of polls. We hear that the percentage of sampled voters in some location who favor candidate X is 45.7%, and this statement is usually accompanied by a "margin of error" of about plus or minus 3%. We are actually being given a 95% confidence interval for the population proportion who favor candidate X: it goes from 0.427 to 0.487. Or we might hear that the percentage of sampled females who favor candidate X is 48.3%, whereas the similar percentage for sampled males is 45.1%. We could then find a 95% confidence interval for the *difference* between the female proportion and the male proportion. It might go from –0.031 to 0.095. (The actual limits depend on the sample size(s).

StatTools 5.5 can calculate such confidence intervals. The analysis is straightforward. The tricky part is the setup of the data set itself. StatTools allows three basic possibilities: (1) a column that indicates which category each sampled

---

[2] This procedure was not available before StatTools 5.5.

member is in, (2) counts of the members in the different categories, and (3) percentages in the different categories. Let's say 1000 voters are sampled, and each expresses a preference for a candidate: Democrat, Republican, or Independent. Then Figure 5.15 indicates the three ways the data might be listed. (See the file **Voter Preferences.xlsx**.) Option 1 lists the preference for each voter (with many rows hidden in the figure); option 2 lists only the counts, and option 3 lists only the percentages. I named these three data sets One-sample List, One-sample Counts, and One-sample Percentages. Note that in option 3, it is also necessary to know the sample size; the percentages alone do not supply this information.

**Figure 5.15**

**Data Setups for Confidence Interval for Proportion**

| | A | B | C | D | E | F | G | H |
|---|---|---|---|---|---|---|---|---|
| 1 | Option 1 | | | Option 2 | | | Option 3 | |
| 2 | | | | | | | | |
| 3 | Voter | Preference | | Preference | Count | | Preference | Count |
| 4 | 1 | Republican | | Democrat | 516 | | Democrat | 51.6% |
| 5 | 2 | Republican | | Republican | 440 | | Republican | 44.0% |
| 6 | 3 | Democrat | | Independent | 44 | | Independent | 4.4% |
| 7 | 4 | Democrat | | | | | | |
| 8 | 5 | Democrat | | | | | Sample size | 1000 |
| 1000 | 997 | Republican | | | | | | |
| 1001 | 998 | Republican | | | | | | |
| 1002 | 999 | Democrat | | | | | | |
| 1003 | 1000 | Republican | | | | | | |

To find a confidence interval for the proportion of all voters in this population who favor the Democrat, select **Confidence Interval for Proportion** from the **Statistical Inference** dropdown and fill in the resulting dialog box as in Figures 15.16, 15.17, or 15.18, depending on which data set you are analyzing. Again, note in Figure 15.18 that I had to supply the sample size toward the bottom.

**Figure 5.16**

**Option 1 Settings: A Data List**

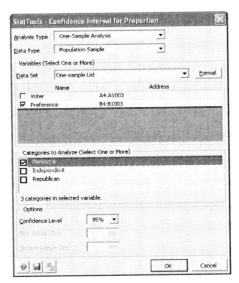

Figure 5.17

Option 2
Settings:
Counts

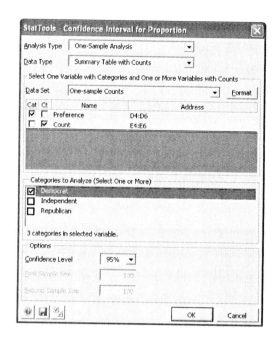

Figure 5.18

Option 3
Settings:
Percentages

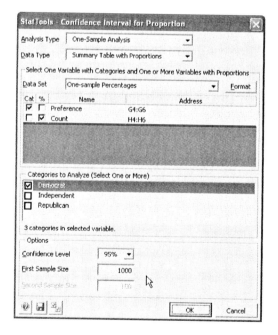

Because these three data sets are all equivalent, the output for each is the same, as shown in Figure 5.19. A 95% confidence interval for the population proportion who favor the Democrat extends from 0.485 to 0.547.

Figure 5.19

Confidence
Interval for
Proportion

| Conf. Interval (Proportion) | Preference One-sample List |
|---|---|
| Category | Democrat |
| Sample Size | 1000 |
| Sample Proportion | 0.516 |
| Confidence Level | 95.0% |
| Standard Error of Proportion | 0.016 |
| Lower Limit | 0.485 |
| Upper Limit | 0.547 |

**Notes**

- Note in the middle of the dialog boxes in Figures 15.16–15.18 that you can check more than one category. StatTools allows you, say, to obtain a confidence interval for the proportion favoring the Democrat *and* a confidence interval favoring the Republican, all in one step.

## Confidence Interval for a Difference Between Proportions[3]

StatTools 5.5 also enables you to calculate a confidence interval for the difference between two proportions. Again, the analysis is straightforward, but you need to be aware of the different data setups you might encounter. Again, there can be a list of all sampled members, a table of counts, or a table of percentages, as shown in Figure 5.20. In the latter two options, you could see either of the two cases shown. If the objective is to compare the female proportion (favoring Democrats, say) to the male proportion, then it is important to realize that the StatTools *variables* are Preference, Male, and Female (and optionally, Total). Therefore, in the top cases, the variables are in columns, whereas in the bottom cases, the variables are in rows. This is important for the settings in the StatTools Data Manager. Also, note that the percentages in option 3 should be for each gender separately. For example, the 53.5% value in cell K4 indicates that 53.5% of all males in the sample favor the Democrat.

Figure 5.20

Data
Setups for
Confidence
Interval for
Difference
Between
Proportions

| | A | B | C | D | E | F | G | H | I | J | K | L | M |
|---|---|---|---|---|---|---|---|---|---|---|---|---|---|
| 1 | Option 1 | | | | Option 2a (variables in columns) | | | | | Option 3a (variables in columns) | | | |
| 2 | | | | | | | | | | | | | |
| 3 | Voter | Gender | Preference | | Preference | Male | Female | Total | | Preference | Male | Female | Total |
| 4 | 1 | Male | Republican | | Democrat | 292 | 224 | 516 | | Democrat | 53.5% | 49.3% | 51.6% |
| 5 | 2 | Male | Republican | | Republican | 229 | 211 | 440 | | Republican | 41.9% | 46.5% | 44.0% |
| 6 | 3 | Male | Democrat | | Independent | 25 | 19 | 44 | | Independent | 4.6% | 4.2% | 4.4% |
| 7 | 4 | Male | Democrat | | | | | | | | | | |
| 8 | 5 | Male | Democrat | | Option 2b (variables in rows) | | | | | Option 3b (variables in rows) | | | |
| 9 | 6 | Female | Democrat | | | | | | | | | | |
| 10 | 7 | Male | Democrat | | Preference | Democrat | Republican | Independent | | Preference | Democrat | Republican | Independent |
| 11 | 8 | Male | Republican | | Male | 292 | 229 | 25 | | Male | 53.5% | 41.9% | 4.6% |
| 12 | 9 | Female | Democrat | | Female | 224 | 211 | 19 | | Female | 49.3% | 46.5% | 4.2% |
| 13 | 10 | Male | Democrat | | Total | 516 | 440 | 44 | | Total | 51.6% | 44.0% | 4.4% |
| 14 | 11 | Male | Democrat | | | | | | | | | | |
| 15 | 12 | Male | Democrat | | | | | | | Sample sizes | Male | Female | |
| 16 | 13 | Male | Republican | | | | | | | | 546 | 454 | |
| 1001 | 998 | Female | Republican | | | | | | | | | | |
| 1002 | 999 | Male | Democrat | | | | | | | | | | |
| 1003 | 1000 | Male | Republican | | | | | | | | | | |

---

[3] This analysis was not available before StatTools 5.5.

To find a confidence interval for the difference between proportions favoring the Democrat (Male minus Female), select **Confidence Interval for Proportion** from the **Statistical Inference** dropdown and fill in the resulting dialog box as in Figure 15.21, 15.22, or 15.23, depending on which data set you are analyzing. Note in Figure 15.23 that I had to supply both sample sizes toward the bottom.

*Figure 5.21*

*Option 1:*
*Data List*

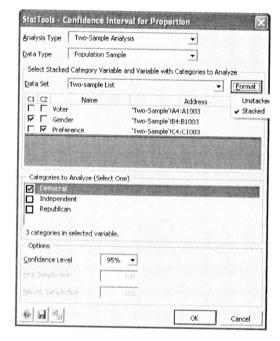

*Figure 5.22*

*Option 2:*
*Counts*

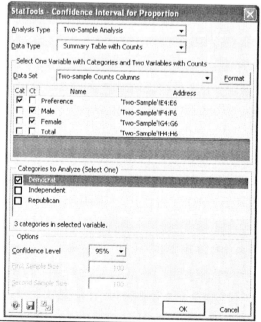

**Figure 5.23**

**Option 3: Percentages**

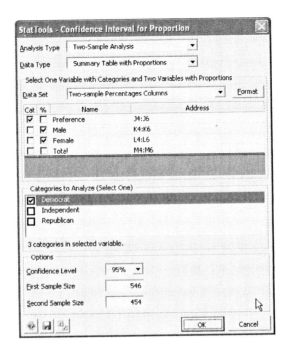

Again, these data sets are equivalent, so the output from each is the same, as shown in Figure 5.24. It implies that we are 95% confident that the difference between the proportions favoring the Democrat (Male minus Female) is between –0.021 and 0.104. Because this includes 0, there is still some doubt about whether females or males are more in favor of the Democrat in the entire population.

**Figure 5.24**

**Confidence Interval for Difference Between Proportions**

| Analyzed Category | | |
|---|---|---|
| Proportion of Items in This Category | Democrat | |
| | | |
| | Preference (Male) | Preference (Female) |
| Sample Summaries | Two-sample List | Two-sample List |
| Sample Size | 546 | 454 |
| Sample Proportion | 0.535 | 0.493 |
| | | |
| Conf. Interval (Difference Between Proportions) | | |
| Confidence Level | 95.0% | |
| Difference Between Proportions | 0.041 | |
| Standard Error of Difference | 0.032 | |
| Lower Limit | -0.021 | |
| Upper Limit | 0.104 | |

**Notes**

- The variable headings in Figure 5.21, C1 and C2, are not very informative. The C1 variable should be the categorical variable whose categories you are comparing, in this case, Gender. The C2 variable should list the categories each voter prefers, in this case Preference.

- If the data are shown as a list, then they are probably in stacked format, as in columns A–C of Figure 5.20. In this case, you have to select the Stacked option in Figure 5.21.

- As usual with comparisons, StatTools asks (in a dialog box not shown here) which difference you want: Male minus Female or the reverse. The difference shown in Figure 5.24 is Male minus Female.

# 5.3 Hypothesis tests[4]

In contrast to confidence intervals, **hypothesis tests** allow you to check whether there is enough evidence in the sample data to conclude, with reasonable assurance, that some prespecified hypothesis, called the **alternative hypothesis**, is true. If there is not enough evidence to make this conclusion, then you cannot reject the opposite hypothesis, called the **null hypothesis**. Almost all hypothesis tests, including those performed by StatTools, calculate a **test statistic**. If this test statistic is sufficiently extreme, as compared to what would be expected under the null hypothesis, then you can conclude that the alternative is true. Accompanying each test statistic is a **p-value**. This is a measure between 0 and 1 that indicates how extreme the test statistic is, with values near 0 indicating more evidence in favor of the alternative. Most statisticians require a p-value to be less than 0.05 before they reject the null, although some use a cutoff of 0.01 or 0.10.

Most hypothesis tests can be either **one-tailed** or **two-tailed**. In general, you need to specify what type of alternative you are trying to prove before running the test. For example, if the alternative is that some difference is not 0, then the test is a two-tailed test, because a large positive *or* a large negative difference provides sufficient evidence to accept the alternative. On the other hand, if the alternative is that some difference is positive, say, then the test is a one-tailed test, because only a large positive difference provides sufficient evidence to accept the alternative.

It is best to think of confidence intervals and hypothesis tests as two complementary procedures for making statistical inferences. Using the same data set, it often makes sense to calculate a confidence interval for a given parameter or test a hypothesis about this parameter. It just depends on the goals of the study. In this section, I will illustrate some of the hypothesis testing procedures of StatTools, using the same data sets as in the discussion of confidence intervals.

## Test for a Mean or Standard Deviation

For the gasoline price data in the file **Gas Prices.xlsx**, we saw that the mean gas price for the 32 gas stations sampled is $3.279. Suppose the goal of the study is to "prove" that the current mean gas price in the entire country is higher than $3.25. The data provide some evidence that this is true, but is it strong enough evidence?

To answer this question, select **Hypothesis Test for Mean/Std. Deviation** from the **Statistical Inference** dropdown and fill in the resulting dialog box as in Figure 5.25. This indicates that we are testing a mean and the alternative hypothesis is that the mean is *greater than* 3.25. Again, the form of the alternative depends entirely on the

---

[4] In StatTools 5.0 and earlier, the menu item for these analyses was simply **Hypothesis Test**. With the addition of hypothesis tests for proportions in version 5.5, the menu item has been renamed to **Hypothesis Test for Mean/Std. Deviation**.

goals of the study. In general, StatTools allows you to specify the alternative as one-tailed (either greater than or less than) or two-tailed (not equal).

Figure 5.25

*Dialog Box for One-Sample Hypothesis Test of the Mean*

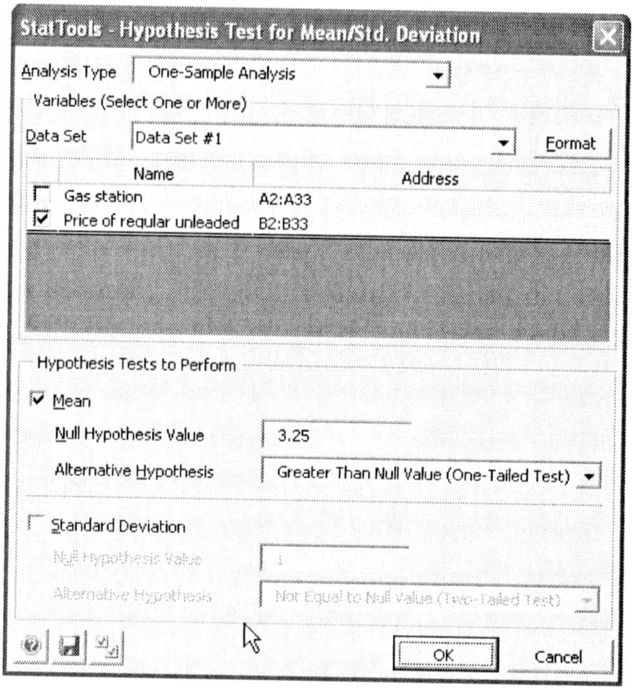

The results appear in Figure 5.26. The test statistic in this case is a **t-statistic** that can be interpreted essentially as the number of standard deviations (really standard *errors*) from the mean. Here, it means that the observed mean is slightly more than 2 standard errors above the mean that we would expect if the null hypothesis were true. Since this is fairly extreme, there is convincing evidence that the true mean is indeed greater than $1.55. This is confirmed by the low p-value of 0.023 and the bottom three messages in the StatTools output. The null hypothesis can be rejected in favor of the alternative at the 10% and 5% significance levels, but the evidence is not quite convincing enough to reject at the 1% level.

Figure 5.26

*Results of Hypothesis Test on the Mean*

| Hypothesis Test (One-Sample) | Price of regular unleaded Data Set #1 |
|---|---|
| Sample Size | 32 |
| Sample Mean | 3.279 |
| Sample Std Dev | 0.079 |
| Hypothesized Mean | 3.25 |
| Alternative Hypothesis | > 3.25 |
| Standard Error of Mean | 0.014 |
| Degrees of Freedom | 31 |
| t-Test Statistic | 2.069 |
| p-Value | 0.0235 |
| Null Hypoth. at 10% Significance | Reject |
| Null Hypoth. at 5% Significance | Reject |
| Null Hypoth. at 1% Significance | Don't Reject |

**Notes**

- As is evident from the dialog box in Figure 5.25, StatTools allows you to test either the mean or the standard deviation — or both — in the one-sample procedure.

## Test for a Difference Between Means: Two-Sample Test

In Section 5.2 we found a confidence interval for the mean difference in satisfaction ratings between men and women for the data in the **Sandwich Ratings.xlsx** file. We saw that the males tended to rate the new sandwich higher than the females. We might hypothesize that this statement is true in the general population. In other words, we want to test whether there is enough evidence in the sample data to conclude that the mean rating for males minus the mean rating for females is greater than 0. (By default, StatTools will analyze the difference Female minus Male because Female comes before Male in alphabetical order. However, it is easy to ask for the reverse, Male minus Female.)

To run this one-tailed test, select **Hypothesis Test for Mean/Std. Deviation** from the **Statistical Inference** dropdown and fill in the resulting dialog box as in Figure 5.27. In particular, select the Two-Sample option from the top dropdown list, and specify the type of alternative as "> 0" in the bottom section. In the next dialog box (not shown here), don't forget to ask for the reverse difference. Based on the alternative hypothesis specified in Figure 5.27, the correct difference to analyze is Male minus Female.

*Figure 5.27*

*Dialog Box for Two-Sample Hypothesis Test*

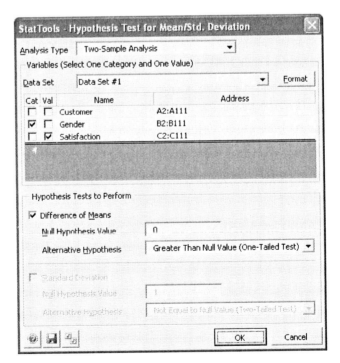

The output from this procedure appears in Figure 5.28. As you see, the sample mean difference (male ratings minus female ratings) is positive, 0.798. This provides some evidence that the alternative hypothesis is true. The test statistic, another t-statistic, and the corresponding p-value indicate that you can reject the null (and accept the alternative) at the 5% or 10% level, but not at the 1% level. The evidence is convincing but not overwhelming. As with two-sample confidence intervals, this test can be run either with or without the assumption of equal population variances. For these data, the right-hand column should be used because the test for equality of variances at the bottom of the output indicates that the variances are *not* equal.

**Figure 5.28**

*Output from Two-Sample Hypothesis Test*

| Sample Summaries | Satisfaction (Male) Data Set #1 | Satisfaction (Female) Data Set #1 |
|---|---|---|
| Sample Size | 71 | 39 |
| Sample Mean | 6.746 | 5.949 |
| Sample Std Dev | 1.787 | 2.470 |
| | | |
| Hypothesis Test (Difference of Means) | Equal Variances | Unequal Variances |
| Hypothesized Mean Difference | 0 | 0 |
| Alternative Hypothesis | > 0 | > 0 |
| Sample Mean Difference | 0.798 | 0.798 |
| Standard Error of Difference | 0.409 | 0.449 |
| Degrees of Freedom | 108 | 60 |
| t-Test Statistic | 1.949 | 1.777 |
| p-Value | 0.0269 | 0.0403 |
| Null Hypoth. at 10% Significance | Reject | Reject |
| Null Hypoth. at 5% Significance | Reject | Reject |
| Null Hypoth. at 1% Significance | Don't Reject | Don't Reject |
| | | |
| Equality of Variances Test | | |
| Ratio of Sample Variances | 0.5231 | |
| p-Value | 0.0190 | |

**Notes**

- When you specify the alternative hypothesis, you can choose from three possibilities in the dropdown list: "less than", "greater than", or "not equal". The first two are for one-tailed tests; the latter is for a two-tailed test. Also, you can specify the null hypothesis value. Its default value is 0, because the test for *equality* of two means is a natural, but it can be any user-specified value.

## Test for a Difference Between Means: Paired-Sample Test

In Section 5.2 we saw how a paired-sample procedure was appropriate for the test results in the **Before-After Tests.xlsx** file. There we saw that the average improvement for the people in the sample was about 30 points. Suppose the developer of the course claims that the mean improvement will be more than 25 points for the population in general. That is, her alternative hypothesis is that the mean after score minus the mean before score is greater than 25.

To run the test, select **Hypothesis Test for Mean/Std. Deviation** from the **Statistical Inference** dropdown and fill in the resulting dialog box as in Figure 5.29. In particular, choose the Paired-Sample option in the top dropdown list and specify the alternative hypothesis as shown.

**Figure 5.29**

**Dialog Box for Paired-Sample Test**

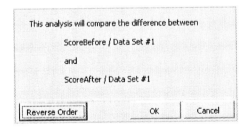

Because you want to test the alternative hypothesis *mean after score minus the mean before score is greater than 25*, select to reverse the order of the test in the **Choose Variable Ordering** dialog that appears in Figure 5.30. Otherwise the mean after score would be subtracted from the mean before score.

**Figure 5.30**

**Reversing the Order of Difference**

This analysis will compare the difference between

ScoreBefore / Data Set #1

and

ScoreAfter / Data Set #1

| Reverse Order | OK | Cancel |

The output from this test appears in Figure 5.31. The t-statistic is quite large in magnitude, and the corresponding p-value is very close to 0. This means that the null hypothesis can be rejected at any of the common significance levels. There is little doubt that the claim of the developer is true—the mean improvement is indeed greater than 25.

Figure 5.31

Output
from
Paired-
Sample
Test

| Hypothesis Test (Paired-Sample) | ScoreAfter - ScoreBefore |
|---|---|
| Sample Size | 28 |
| Sample Mean | 30 5 |
| Sample Std Dev | 6 586 |
| Hypothesized Mean | 25 |
| Alternative Hypothesis | > 25 |
| Standard Error of Mean | 1.245 |
| Degrees of Freedom | 27 |
| t-Test Statistic | 4.419 |
| p-Value | < 0 0001 |
| Null Hypoth. at 10% Significance | Reject |
| Null Hypoth. at 5% Significance | Reject |
| Null Hypoth. at 1% Significance | Reject |

## Test for a Proportion[5]

In Section 5.2, we found a confidence interval for the proportion of voters who favor the Democrat candidate. (See the file **Voter Preferences.xlsx**.) It is also possible to test a hypothesis for this proportion. Here, I will test the alternative hypothesis that the population proportion who favor the Democrat is at least 50%. Given that the sample proportion favoring the Democrat is 51.6%, there is evidence that the alternative is true, but is it strong enough evidence?

To run this test, select **Hypothesis Test for Proportion** from the **Statistical Inference** dropdown and fill in the resulting dialog box as shown in Figure 5.32. (This is for the data set where the individual voter preferences are listed in a column, but the same analysis can be done for any of the other "proportion" data setups discussed in Section 5.2.)

Figure 5.32

Dialog Box
for Test of
Proportion

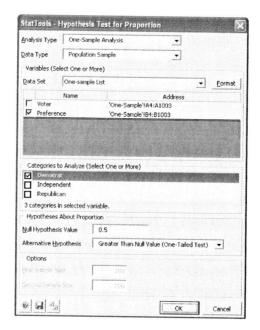

---

[5] This analysis was not available before StatTools 5.5.

The resulting output appears in Figure 5.33. Perhaps surprisingly, in spite of a sample proportion of 51.6% and a "large" sample size of 1000, the null hypothesis cannot be rejected, even at the 10% significance level.

**Figure 5.33**

**Test of Proportion**

| Hypothesis Test (Proportion) | Preference One-sample List |
|---|---|
| Category | Democrat |
| Sample Size | 1000 |
| Sample Proportion | 0.516 |
| Hypothesized Proportion | 0.5 |
| Alternative Hypothesis | > 0.5 |
| Standard Error of Sample Proportion | 0.016 |
| z-Test Statistic | 1.0119 |
| p-Value | 0.1558 |
| Null Hypoth. at 10% Significance | Don't Reject |
| Null Hypoth. at 5% Significance | Don't Reject |
| Null Hypoth. at 1% Significance | Don't Reject |

## Test for a Difference Between Proportions[6]

Similarly, it is possible test a difference between proportions. Again drawing on the data in the **Voter Preferences.xlsx** file, we saw that 53.5% of the males favored the Democrat, whereas only 49.3% of the females favored the Democrat. Is this enough evidence to accept the alternative hypothesis that a higher proportion of males favor the Democrat than females?

To run this test, select **Hypothesis Test for Proportion** from the **Statistical Inference** dropdown and fill in the resulting dialog box as shown in Figure 5.34. (This is for the data set where the individual voter preferences are listed in a column, but the same analysis can be done for any of the other "proportion" data setups discussed in Section 5.2.)

---

[6] This analysis was not available before StatTools 5.5.

Figure 5.34

Dialog Box
for Test of
Difference
Between
Proportions

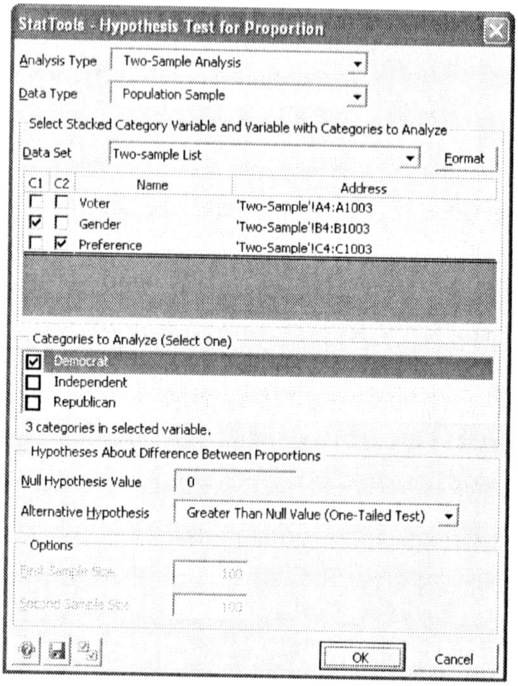

The resulting output appears in Figure 5.35. The p-value is 0.096, so there is enough evidence to accept the alternative at the 10% level, but not at the 5% or 1% levels.

Figure 5.35

Test of
Difference
Between
Proportions

| Analyzed Category | | |
|---|---|---|
| Proportion of Items in This Category | Democrat | |
| | Preference (Male) | Preference (Female) |
| Sample Summaries | Two-sample List | Two-sample List |
| Sample Size | 546 | 454 |
| Sample Proportion | 0.535 | 0.493 |
| Hypothesis Test (Difference Between Proportions) | | |
| Pooled Proportion | 0.516 | |
| Difference Between Proportions | 0.041 | |
| Hypothesized Difference | 0 | |
| Alternative Hypothesis | > 0 | |
| Standard Error of Difference | 0.032 | |
| Test Statistic | 1.3045 | |
| p-Value | 0.0960 | |
| Null Hypoth. at 10% Significance | Reject | |
| Null Hypoth. at 5% Significance | Don't Reject | |
| Null Hypoth. at 1% Significance | Don't Reject | |

# 5.4 Sample Size Selection

When a statistical procedure calculates a confidence interval from given data, it typically calculates a point estimate, such as a sample mean, and then goes out about two standard errors on either side of the point estimate to get the endpoints of the confidence interval. Therefore, the standard error determines the length of the confidence interval, and it can typically be reduced only by increasing the sample size. This is typically done at the planning stage. You specify the length of the confidence interval you would like, and then you find the sample size(s) required to achieve\this length. Fortunately, there are sample size formulas available in common situations, and StatTools implements these.

Note that no data sets are required in these sample size procedures. Because sample sizes are selected in the planning stages, the sample size formulas cannot rely on data that have not yet been collected. However, the sample size formulas do require some estimates of parameters from the population distribution. For example, the sample size formula for estimating a mean requires an estimate of the population standard deviation. This estimate is usually a "best guess," possibly based on historical data or a small pilot study.

## Confidence Interval for a Mean

In estimating the mean price of regular unleaded gasoline in Section 5.2, we saw that the 32 observations in the file **Gas Prices.xlsx** lead to the 95% confidence interval 3.279 plus or minus 0.029. We say that the **half-length** of this interval is 0.029. If you want to decrease this half-length to, say, 0.005, what sample size is required?

To answer this question, select **Sample Size Selection** from the **Statistical Inference** dropdown and fill in the resulting dialog box as in Figure 5.36. (Again, no data set is required, but a workbook must be open; otherwise, StatTools will give an error message.) In particular, you need to specify the confidence level, the desired half-length, and an *estimate* of the standard deviation. Here I have used 0.08 to estimate this standard deviation, because this is approximately the sample standard deviation in the original data set. (In real applications, a small pilot experiment is often undertaken to provide this estimate.)

**Figure 5.36**

*Sample
Size Dialog
Box for a
Mean*

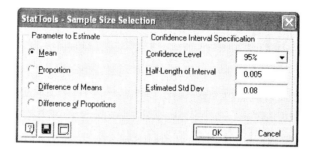

The results appear in Figure 5.37. The claim is that if a 95% confidence interval for the mean is based on a sample 984 gas stations, the resulting half-length will be about 0.005. Be aware, however, that the actual half-length could be less than or greater than 0.005. It all depends on how the observed standard deviation compares to the estimate you provide.

**Figure 5.37**

*Required
Sample
Size for
Estimating
the Mean*

| Sample Size for Mean | |
|---|---|
| Confidence Level | 95% |
| Half-length of Interval | 0.005 |
| Std Dev (estimate) | 0.080 |
| Sample Size | 984 |

### Notes

- Sometimes the required sample size is too large to be practical. Then you must typically settle for a longer confidence interval than you would like.

## Confidence Interval for a Proportion

Suppose you want to estimate a proportion, such as the proportion of all adults who have watched the show Mad Men. You would like the resulting 95% confidence interval to be of the form $x \pm 0.03$, that is, a confidence interval with a half-length of 0.03, centered at the point estimate $x$. (Any half-length could be chosen. I have chosen 0.03 because new shows often quote a "sampling error of plus or minus 3%." This translates to a half-length of 0.03.)

To find the required sample size, select **Sample Size Selection** from the **Statistical Inference** dropdown and fill in the dialog box as in Figure 5.38. Note that an estimate of the population proportion is required—in this case, the proportion of all adults who have watched the show. Of course, you don't know this proportion—it is the proportion you are trying to estimate in the first place!—but you guess that it is somewhere around 0.3. The results in Figure 5.39 indicate that a sample 897 adults is required to obtain the desired accuracy.

**Figure 5.38**

*Sample Size Dialog Box for Proportion*

**Figure 5.39**

*Required Sample Size for Estimating Proportion*

| Sample Size for Proportion | |
|---|---|
| Confidence Level | 95% |
| Half-length of Interval | 0.03 |
| Proportion (estimate) | 0.30 |
| Sample Size | 897 |

### Notes

- If you have no idea of the proportion, it is common to use 0.5 as an estimate in the dialog box. This results in a sample size that is certainly large enough to produce the desired half-length, regardless of the true proportion.

- The following requirements hold:

  *Estimated Proportion – Half Length > 0*
  *Estimated Proportion + Half Length < 1.*

## Confidence Interval for a Difference Between Means

Using the data on satisfaction ratings in the file **Sandwich Ratings.xlsx**, we found a 95% confidence interval for the mean female rating minus the mean male rating to be –0.798 plus or minus 0.898 $-0.798 \pm 0.898$. This was based on sample sizes of 39 females and 71 males. In this case, if you want to reduce the length of the confidence interval, the usual procedure is to select a *common* sample size for males and females. Also, you must specify an estimate of the (assumed) common standard deviation for each group.

Suppose you want to reduce the half-length to 0.5, and you believe the common standard deviation of ratings for both males and females is approximately 2.0. (This is a compromise between the sample standard deviations observed earlier.) Then select **Sample Size Selection** from the **Statistical Inference** dropdown and fill in the dialog box as in Figure 5.40. The results in Figure 5.41 indicate that samples of 123 females and 123 males are required. Then if the standard deviation of ratings for each gender is approximately 2.0, the resulting 95% confidence interval for the difference between means will have a half-length near 0.5.

*Figure 5.40*

*Sample
Size Dialog
Box for
Difference
Between
Means*

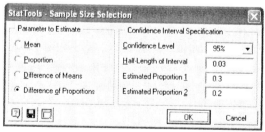

*Figure 5.41*

*Required
Common
Sample
Size for
Estimating
Difference
Between
Means*

| Sample Size for Difference of Means | |
|---|---|
| Confidence Level | 95% |
| Half-length of Interval | 0.50 |
| Common Std Dev (estimate) | 2.00 |
| Sample Size | 123 |

## Confidence Interval for a Difference Between Proportions

Suppose you want a confidence interval for the difference between the proportion of male adults who have watched the show Mad Men and the similar proportion of female adults. You want this confidence interval to have the form $x \pm 0.03$, so that it has half-length 0.03 and is centered at the point estimate $x$ of the difference between the two proportions. As with estimating the difference between means, the typical practice is to find a common sample size for each gender that will produce the required accuracy.

To find this common sample size, select **Sample Size Selection** from the **Statistical Inference** dropdown and fill in the dialog box as in Figure 5.42. Note that estimates of *both* proportions are required. (The ones used here are best guesses.) The results in Figure 5.43 indicate that samples of 1580 males and 1580 females are required to obtain the desired accuracy.

*Figure 5.42*

*Sample
Size Dialog
Box for
Difference
Between
Proportions*

**Figure 5.43**

**Required Common Sample Size for Estimating Difference Between Proportions**

| Sample Size for Difference of Proportions | |
|---|---|
| Confidence Level | 95% |
| Half-length of Interval | 0.03 |
| Proportion 1 | 0.30 |
| Proportion 2 | 0.20 |
| Sample Size | 1580 |

## Notes

- If you have no idea of the two proportions, it is common to use 0.5 as an estimate for each of them in the dialog box. This results in a common sample size that is certainly large enough to produce the desired half-length, regardless of the actual proportions.

# 5.5 Analysis of Variance (ANOVA)

Analysis of variance (ANOVA) is a group of procedures for testing whether means differ across groups. It is part of the larger topic of **experimental design**, an extremely important topic in applied statistics. Indeed, large statistical software packages such as SPSS and SAS have a bewildering variety of ANOVA-type procedures. StatTools includes only the two simplest (and probably most frequently used) versions of ANOVA: one-way ANOVA and two-way ANOVA

## One-Way ANOVA

I have already discussed the two-sample procedure for testing whether the means from two groups are equal. To extend this test to three or more groups, the appropriate procedure is **one-way analysis of variance (ANOVA)**. One-way ANOVA lets you test whether the means from three or more groups are all equal. The alternative hypothesis is that at least one of the means is different from at least one of the others. In case the p-value for the test is small, indicating that the means are *not* all equal, it is then useful to look at confidence intervals of differences between pairs of means. In this way, you can see which means are significantly different from which others.

When you create, say, 95% confidence intervals for several pairs of means, it is difficult to determine the overall confidence level of the test — that is, the confidence level that *all* of the intervals include their corresponding true mean differences. This overall confidence level is *not* necessarily 95%, at least not unless the confidence interval formulas are modified. There are several methods that have been proposed to achieve the *correct* overall confidence level. StatTools implements four confidence interval procedures. These include the **No correction** method, which is the usual two-sample confidence interval from Section 5.2, and the **Tukey, Bonferroni**, and **Scheffe** methods. The latter three methods typically give similar results. For technical reasons, the Tukey method is often the method of choice.

There are actually many versions of analysis of variance. The purpose of all of them is to detect mean differences between different groups, often in some type of experimental design setting. The one-way ANOVA procedure implemented in StatTools is the simplest version. It assumes that (1) the samples from the different groups are statistically independent, (2) the population variances of the various groups are the same, and (3) the observations in each group are normally distributed. These assumptions should be checked for plausibility before trusting the one-way ANOVA results.

To illustrate one-way ANOVA, consider the data in Figure 5.44. This data set is the result of an experiment where five brands of golf balls were all driven by a mechanical machine under identical conditions and the distances (in yards) were recorded. (Only a portion of the data appears here. There are actually 15 observations for each brand. The entire data set is in the file **Golf Ball 1.xlsx**.) Is there evidence that some brands go farther than others? If so, which are significantly different from which others?

**Figure 5.44**

**Golf Ball Data**

| | A | B |
|---|---|---|
| 1 | Brand | Distance |
| 2 | A | 270.6 |
| 3 | B | 271.3 |
| 4 | C | 292.8 |
| 5 | D | 272.5 |
| 6 | E | 240.4 |
| 7 | A | 277.5 |
| 8 | B | 263.1 |
| 9 | C | 296.0 |
| 10 | D | 261.5 |

To answer these questions, select **One-Way ANOVA** from the **Statistical Inference** dropdown and fill in the resulting dialog box as in Figure 5.45, making sure to indicate that the data are in stacked form (one column for brand identification and one for distance). For illustration, I checked two of the four confidence interval methods, although you can check any number of these options.

**Figure 5.45**

**Dialog Box for One-Way ANOVA**

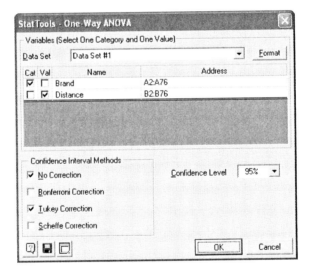

The results appear in Figure 5.46. The Sample Mean row of the ANOVA Sample Stats section indicates that the sample means vary from a low of 253.8 to a high of 284.5. This appears to be a lot of variation across brands, and it is confirmed by the ANOVA table. This ANOVA table runs the test for equal means. Its test statistic is an **F-ratio**, where larger F-ratios are more convincing evidence of unequal means. The corresponding p-value is virtually 0, which leaves little doubt that the 5 brands do *not* all result in the same mean distance.

**Figure 5.46**

**Results for One-Way ANOVA**

| ANOVA Summary | |
|---|---|
| Total Sample Size | 75 |
| Grand Mean | 268.33 |
| Pooled Std Dev | 7.45 |
| Pooled Variance | 55.53 |
| Number of Samples | 5 |
| Confidence Level | 95.00% |

| ANOVA Sample Stats | Distance (A) Data Set #1 | Distance (B) Data Set #1 | Distance (C) Data Set #1 | Distance (D) Data Set #1 | Distance (E) Data Set #1 |
|---|---|---|---|---|---|
| Sample Size | 15 | 15 | 15 | 15 | 15 |
| Sample Mean | 270.29 | 260.66 | 284.49 | 272.41 | 253.81 |
| Sample Std Dev | 3.95 | 6.97 | 8.38 | 9.29 | 7.54 |
| Sample Variance | 15.64 | 48.63 | 70.28 | 86.23 | 56.88 |
| Pooling Weight | 0.2000 | 0.2000 | 0.2000 | 0.2000 | 0.2000 |

| OneWay ANOVA Table | Sum of Squares | Degrees of Freedom | Mean Squares | F-Ratio | p-Value |
|---|---|---|---|---|---|
| Between Variation | 8270.16 | 4 | 2067.54 | 37.23 | < 0.0001 |
| Within Variation | 3887.17 | 70 | 55.53 | | |
| Total Variation | 12157.33 | 74 | | | |

| Confidence Interval Tests | Difference of Means | No Correction Lower | No Correction Upper | Tukey Lower | Tukey Upper |
|---|---|---|---|---|---|
| Distance (A)-Distance (B) | 9.63 | 4.206 | 15.060 | 2.012 | 17.255 |
| Distance (A)-Distance (C) | -14.20 | -19.627 | -8.773 | -21.822 | -6.578 |
| Distance (A)-Distance (D) | -2.12 | -7.547 | 3.307 | -9.742 | 5.502 |
| Distance (A)-Distance (E) | 16.48 | 11.053 | 21.907 | 8.858 | 24.102 |
| Distance (B)-Distance (C) | -23.83 | -29.260 | -18.406 | -31.455 | -16.212 |
| Distance (B)-Distance (D) | -11.75 | -17.180 | -6.326 | -19.375 | -4.132 |
| Distance (B)-Distance (E) | 6.85 | 1.420 | 12.274 | -0.775 | 14.468 |
| Distance (C)-Distance (D) | 12.08 | 6.653 | 17.507 | 4.458 | 19.702 |
| Distance (C)-Distance (E) | 30.68 | 25.253 | 36.107 | 23.058 | 38.302 |
| Distance (D)-Distance (E) | 18.60 | 13.173 | 24.027 | 10.978 | 26.222 |

The confidence intervals at the bottom of the output indicate which means are different from which others. Specifically, if a confidence interval is all positive or all negative — meaning that a difference of 0 is not very plausible — then StatTools boldfaces the interval. For example, the confidence interval for the difference between brands A and C is all negative and hence boldfaced, indicating that brand A results in significantly less distance than brand C. In contrast, the confidence interval for the difference between brands A and D extends from negative to positive, so it is not boldfaced. This indicates that there is no significant difference between these two brands.

Note that there are 10 possible differences, the number of ways 2 brands can be chosen from 5 brands total. With this many confidence intervals being reported, it is safer to rely on Tukey's method, which produces slightly longer confidence intervals than the No correction method. Because of these longer intervals, Tukey's method sometimes reports that a difference is not significant (see the comparison of brands B and E), when the No correction method reports that it is significant.

**Notes**

- The data for one-way ANOVA can be in stacked or unstacked form; StatTools will accept either—unlike some statistical packages, which require stacked data. Also, the sample sizes are *not* required to be equal. However, equal sample sizes are preferable when possible (see the following bullet point).

- The independence across groups is a reasonable assumption in this golf ball experiment, but the equal-variance and normality assumptions are more suspect. Fortunately, the one-way ANOVA procedure is fairly robust with respect to violations of these assumptions, especially when the sample sizes are equal, as they are in the golf ball data set.

## Two-Way ANOVA

In the golf ball experiment in the previous section, we saw how the mean distance varies with brand. In ANOVA terminology, brand is called a **factor**, and the values of the factor (A, B, and so on) are called its **treatment levels**, or simply **levels**. In this case, there are five levels, corresponding to the five brands. The *one* in one-way ANOVA means that there is a single factor. It is also possible to vary two factors in an experiment. This requires a **two-way ANOVA** procedure. If observations are made for each combination of levels of the two factors, it is called a **full-factorial design**. If, in addition, the number of observations is the same for each combination of levels, it is called a **balanced design**.

StatTools implements only the simplest of the many possible two-factor experimental designs: the full-factorial balanced design. This means, for example, that if there are 3 levels of one factor and 4 levels of the other factor, there must be an equal number of observations for each of the 12 combinations of levels. If this common sample size is 10, say, then there will be 120 observations total. In addition, StatTools requires that the data be in stacked form. This means that there must be two *category* variables, each indicating the level of a factor, and a *value* variable, indicating a measurement.

To see how two-way ANOVA works, consider the data in Figure 5.47. (This is actually just a small portion of the full data set in the file **Golf Ball 2.xlsx**). Each of 5 brands (A–E) was driven in each of 3 temperatures (cool, mild, and warm) 20 times, for a total of 300 observations. The purpose of the study is to see whether any brands dominate others in terms of distance. However, a secondary objective is to see whether this brand effect depends on temperature.

Figure 5.47

Golf Ball
Data with
Two
Factors

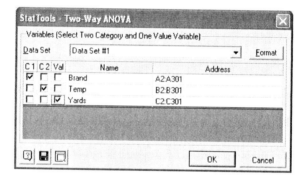

|  | A | B | C |
|---|---|---|---|
| 1 | Brand | Temp | Yards |
| 2 | A | Cool | 220.6 |
| 3 | A | Cool | 204.0 |
| 4 | A | Cool | 233.6 |
| 5 | A | Cool | 229.1 |
| 6 | A | Cool | 214.6 |
| 7 | A | Cool | 208.8 |
| 8 | A | Cool | 204.6 |
| 9 | A | Cool | 219.2 |
| 10 | A | Cool | 208.0 |

To analyze this data set, select **Two-Way ANOVA** from the **Statistical Inference** dropdown and fill in the resulting dialog box as in Figure 5.48. There aren't many choices here. Only a stacked format is allowed, and you must select two categorical (C1 and C2) variables and one value variable.

Figure 5.48

Dialog Box
for Two-
Way
ANOVA

The output comes in two parts: numerical and graphical. The numerical output appears in Figure 5.49. This indicates that the sample sizes are indeed identical. It also provides a table of sample means and a table of sample standard deviations. The latter is useful for checking an assumption of two-way ANOVA: equal variances. (For these data, unequal variances does not appear to be a problem.) The table of sample means is of most interest. It indicates that distances tend to increase as the temperature increases—no surprise to any golfer. More importantly, by comparing the rows of this table, you can compare brands. The totals to the right are averages over the different temperatures. They indicate that, on average, brand E is the longest ball and brand D is the shortest. However, the middle three columns for the separate temperatures do not necessarily exhibit the same pattern as the Totals column. In fact, this is one of the main questions in such a study, as discussed below.

**Figure 5.49**

**Numerical
Two-Way
ANOVA
Output**

| ANOVA Sample Sizes | Cool | Mild | Warm | Totals |
|---|---|---|---|---|
| A | 20 | 20 | 20 | 60 |
| B | 20 | 20 | 20 | 60 |
| C | 20 | 20 | 20 | 60 |
| D | 20 | 20 | 20 | 60 |
| E | 20 | 20 | 20 | 60 |
| Totals | 100 | 100 | 100 | |
| Balanced | TRUE | | | |

| ANOVA Sample Means | Cool | Mild | Warm | Totals |
|---|---|---|---|---|
| A | 218.82 | 236.45 | 258.44 | 237.90 |
| B | 224.15 | 245.13 | 258.27 | 242.52 |
| C | 228.00 | 242.72 | 263.04 | 244.58 |
| D | 215.00 | 237.62 | 256.11 | 236.24 |
| E | 224.79 | 255.75 | 270.94 | 250.49 |
| Totals | 222.15 | 243.53 | 261.36 | |

| ANOVA Sample Std Dev | Cool | Mild | Warm | Totals |
|---|---|---|---|---|
| A | 10.90 | 8.83 | 11.01 | 19.22 |
| B | 11.70 | 9.80 | 8.93 | 17.36 |
| C | 10.85 | 14.25 | 7.08 | 18.15 |
| D | 13.64 | 10.18 | 12.13 | 20.69 |
| E | 10.67 | 10.96 | 9.05 | 21.84 |
| Totals | 12.28 | 12.78 | 10.98 | |

| TwoWay ANOVA Table | Sum of Squares | Degrees of Freedom | Mean Squares | F-Ratio | p-Value |
|---|---|---|---|---|---|
| Brand | 7702.44 | 4 | 1925.61 | 16.47 | < 0.0001 |
| Temp | 77086.00 | 2 | 38543.00 | 329.58 | < 0.0001 |
| Interaction | 1999.97 | 8 | 250.00 | 2.14 | 0.0325 |
| Error | 33329.13 | 285 | 116.94 | | |
| Total | 120117.53 | 299 | | | |

The bottom section, the ANOVA table, reports three tests. The top two are for the **main effects** of brand and temperature. For example, the test for the main effect of brand is basically a test of whether the means for the various brands, after averaging over the various temperatures, are equal. Because of their very small p-values, you can conclude that brand indeed makes a difference, as does temperature. The third test is for **interactions**, where an interaction indicates that the effect of one factor depends on the level of the other factor. For example, one possible interaction is that one brand is best in warm weather, whereas another brand is best in cool weather. The small p-value for interactions indicates that there are indeed statistically significant interactions. However, you must investigate further to see what types of interactions are present.

The graphs in Figures 5.50 and 5.51, produced automatically by the StatTools two-way ANOVA procedure, let you examine the interactions. (I changed the scale on the vertical axes to make the lines fill the graphs better.) The first graph shows how average distance varies by temperature for each of the brands. The second shows how average distance varies by brand for each of the temperatures. These two graphs are completely equivalent; they simply provide two alternative ways to view the data. If there were no interactions, the lines in either of these graphs would be parallel, indicating that temperature doesn't affect the relationship between distance and brand, and brand doesn't affect the relationship between distance and temperature. The lines in these graphs are not exactly parallel. For example, brand E is best in mild and warm temperatures, but brand C is slightly better than brand E in cool temperatures. Nevertheless, it is doubtful that the interactions seen here are of much practical importance to golfers. Granted, they are statistically significant, but they are probably not of much practical importance.

*Figure 5.50*

**One Graph of Interactions**

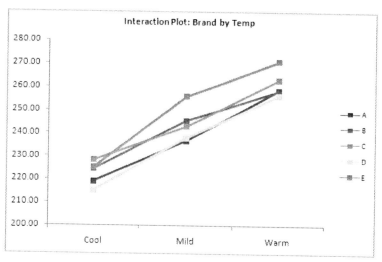

*Figure 5.51*

**Another Graph of Interactions**

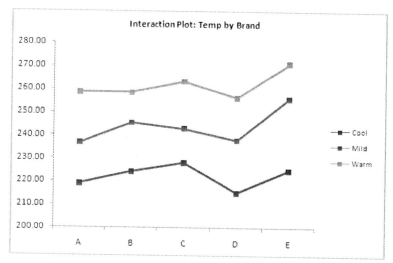

# 5.6 Chi-Square Independence Test

Do people who drink more alcohol tend to smoke more cigarettes? This is a typical question addressed by the **chi-square test for independence** discussed here. To obtain the data for this test, each behavior, drinking and smoking, is divided into categories, and counts of a sample of people are obtained for all of the joint categories. For example, one joint category might be "heavy drinker and nonsmoker." These counts are displayed in a table called a **contingency table** (or a **crosstabs** or a **pivot table**). The data set in Figure 5.52 (see the file **Smoking-Drinking.xlsx**) illustrates one possible contingency table. It is obtained by observing 623 people and classifying each person into one of 16 smoking–drinking categories. These tables are often accompanied by row and column totals, as shown here.

*Figure 5.52*

*Contingency Table for Smoking and Drinking*

| | A | B | C | D | E | F | G |
|---|---|---|---|---|---|---|---|
| 1 | | | Smoking category | | | | |
| 2 | | | Non | Light | Moderate | Heavy | Totals |
| 3 | Drinking | Non | 113 | 27 | 21 | 44 | 205 |
| 4 | category | Light | 69 | 53 | 27 | 14 | 163 |
| 5 | | Moderate | 44 | 32 | 19 | 25 | 120 |
| 6 | | Heavy | 37 | 34 | 17 | 47 | 135 |
| 7 | | Totals | 263 | 146 | 84 | 130 | 623 |

To understand the concept of independence versus its opposite, dependence, note that 263 of the 623 people, or 42.2%, are nonsmokers. Also, for example, 113 of 205 nondrinkers, or 55.1%, are nonsmokers, and 37 of 135 heavy drinkers, or 27.4%, are nonsmokers. Each of these statements quotes the percentage of some group who are nonsmokers. If smoking and drinking are independent, these percentages should be the same. Of course, because of random variation in the samples observed, these percentages will probably not be *exactly* the same, but they should be close. Otherwise, there is evidence that some form of *dependence* exists. The chi-square test lets you test this formally, using dependence as the alternative hypothesis.

To run this test, select **Chi-Square Independence Test** from the **Statistical Inference** dropdown and fill in the resulting dialog box as in Figure 5.53. Note that this StatTools procedure does *not* use a predefined data set like most of the other procedures. Instead, you need to specify the range where the contingency table lives, without the row and column totals but (optionally) with the category labels (the row and column headers) and possibly columns and rows titles. (It is a good idea to use the row and column headers because they are then used as labels in the StatTools output.)

---

*Figure 5.53*

*Dialog Box for Chi-Square Independence Test*

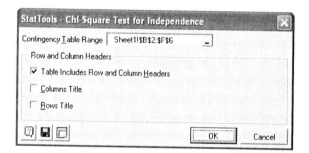

The output appears in Figure 5.. For comparison, the counts are expressed as percentages of row totals and as percentages of column totals. Under independence, the rows in the Percentage of Rows section should be identical, and the columns in the Percentage of Columns section should be identical. The rest of the output lists intermediate results that are used to calculate the **chi-square test statistic** near the bottom. If this statistic is large, there is evidence of dependence. Equivalently, a *small* p-value is an indication of dependence. With this data set, the p-value is virtually 0, so there is little doubt that smoking and drinking habits are *not* independent. Indeed, a close look at the various percentages in the output indicates that smoking and drinking tend to go together.

## Notes

- If there are two row categories and two column categories, this chi-square test is very similar to the test for a difference between proportions discussed in Section 5.3. For example, it could test whether the proportion of heavy drinkers among the heavy smokers is different from the proportion of heavy drinkers amoung the nonsmokers. However, the test from Section 5.3 has the advantage that it can be either one-tailed or two-tailed, whereas the chi-square test is basically two-tailed.

**Figure 5.54**

*Output for Chi-Square Independence Test*

| Original Counts | Rows: Drinking / Columns: Smoking | | | | |
|---|---|---|---|---|---|
| | Non | Light | Moderate | Heavy | Total |
| Non | 113 | 27 | 21 | 44 | 205 |
| Light | 69 | 53 | 27 | 14 | 163 |
| Moderate | 44 | 32 | 19 | 25 | 120 |
| Heavy | 37 | 34 | 17 | 47 | 135 |
| Total | 263 | 146 | 84 | 130 | 623 |

| Percentage of Rows | Rows: Drinking / Columns: Smoking | | | | |
|---|---|---|---|---|---|
| | Non | Light | Moderate | Heavy | |
| Non | 55.12% | 13.17% | 10.24% | 21.46% | 100.00% |
| Light | 42.33% | 32.52% | 16.56% | 8.59% | 100.00% |
| Moderate | 36.67% | 26.67% | 15.83% | 20.83% | 100.00% |
| Heavy | 27.41% | 25.19% | 12.59% | 34.81% | 100.00% |

| Percentage of Columns | Rows: Drinking / Columns: Smoking | | | |
|---|---|---|---|---|
| | Non | Light | Moderate | Heavy |
| Non | 42.97% | 18.49% | 25.00% | 33.85% |
| Light | 26.24% | 36.30% | 32.14% | 10.77% |
| Moderate | 16.73% | 21.92% | 22.62% | 19.23% |
| Heavy | 14.07% | 23.29% | 20.24% | 36.15% |
| | 100.00% | 100.00% | 100.00% | 100.00% |

| Expected Counts | Rows: Drinking / Columns: Smoking | | | |
|---|---|---|---|---|
| | Non | Light | Moderate | Heavy |
| Non | 86.5409 | 48.0417 | 27.6404 | 42.7769 |
| Light | 68.8106 | 38.1990 | 21.9775 | 34.0128 |
| Moderate | 50.6581 | 28.1220 | 16.1798 | 25.0401 |
| Heavy | 56.9904 | 31.6372 | 18.2022 | 28.1701 |

| Distance from Expected | Rows: Drinking / Columns: Smoking | | | |
|---|---|---|---|---|
| | Non | Light | Moderate | Heavy |
| Non | 8.0896 | 9.2160 | 1.5953 | 0.0350 |
| Light | 0.0005 | 5.7349 | 1.1478 | 11.7754 |
| Moderate | 0.8751 | 0.5348 | 0.4916 | 0.0001 |
| Heavy | 7.0120 | 0.1765 | 0.0794 | 12.5865 |

| Chi-Square Statistic | |
|---|---|
| Chi-Square | 59.3504 |
| p-Value | < 0.0001 |

# Chapter 6: Normality Tests

## 6.1 Introduction

**Normality
Tests Icon**

Because so many statistical procedures assume that a variable is normally distributed, it is useful to have methods that check this assumption. StatTools provides three commonly used procedures that are described in this chapter. The first two of these are formal hypothesis tests, where the null hypothesis is that the distribution is normal, and the alternative is that it is *any* nonnormal distribution. Because of the way hypothesis tests work, this means that the burden of proof is on showing that a distribution is *not* normal. In other words, you continue to accept the null hypothesis of normality unless you see convincing evidence to the contrary. The **power** of the test measures how well it is able to detect nonnormal distributions. The first test below is typically less powerful than the second. The third procedure provided by StatTools is not a formal hypothesis test, but it provides graphical evidence of whether a distribution is normal.

## 6.2 Chi-Square Test  *fo- NORMALITY*

In general, a **chi-square goodness-of-fit test** checks whether the *observed* counts in various categories match the *expected* counts based on some null hypothesis. For this particular chi-square test of normality, the range of data is divided into categories, and a count is obtained of the observations in each category. Then these counts are compared to those expected for a normal distribution with the same mean and standard deviation as in the sample. If the two sets of counts match reasonably well, the normality assumption is plausible. Otherwise, there is evidence of nonnormality. Specifically, the null hypothesis of normality is rejected when the chi-square test statistic is large, or equivalently, when the corresponding p-value is small.

To illustrate the procedures in this chapter, consider the data shown in Figure 6.1 on part widths at a manufacturing plant. (There are actually 90 observations. The full data set is in the file **Part Widths.xlsx**.) Before making any formal tests, it is useful to create a histogram (discussed in Chapter 4) to see the shape of the distribution. This histogram, shown in Figure 6.2, looks reasonably bell-shaped, but it is difficult to "eye-ball" how well it really resembles a normal curve.

*Figure 6.1*

*Data on
Part Widths*

| | A | B |
|---|---|---|
| 1 | Part | Width |
| 2 | 1 | 9.990 |
| 3 | 2 | 10.031 |
| 4 | 3 | 9.985 |
| 5 | 4 | 9.983 |
| 6 | 5 | 10.004 |
| 7 | 6 | 10.000 |
| 8 | 7 | 9.992 |
| 9 | 8 | 9.996 |
| 10 | 9 | 9.997 |
| 11 | 10 | 9.993 |

*Figure 6.2*

*Histogram
of Part
Width Data*

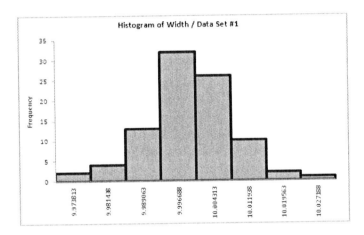

To check normality formally, select **Chi-Square Test** from the **Normality Tests** dropdown and accept the defaults in the resulting dialog box shown in Figure 6.3. Note that because this test is essentially a comparison of histograms (actual versus normal), StatTools asks for the same type of bin information as in its histogram procedure. Although you can specify your own bins, it is perfectly acceptable to use the StatTools default bins.

Figure 6.3

Dialog Box
for Chi-
Square Test

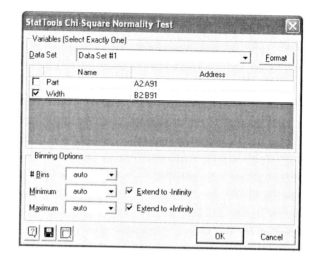

The output comes in two parts, shown in Figures 6.4 and 6.5. The first of these is for the hypothesis test. It shows the chi-square test statistic and the corresponding p-value. Because this p-value is not at all small, the normality hypothesis cannot be rejected at any of the usual significance levels. The table and graph in Figure 6.5 support this conclusion. The graph shows the histogram of the data, with a normal histogram superimposed. They are quite similar—or at least not sufficiently *dissimilar* to reject the hypothesis of normality.

Figure 6.4

Output for
Hypothesis
Test

| Chi-Square Test | Width Data Set #1 |
|---|---|
| Mean | 9.999256 |
| Std Dev | 0.009728 |
| Chi-Square Stat. | 4.2027 |
| P-Value | 0.5206 |

*because test assumes N so have to prove is non-normal → if p = 0.05, means sig chance is non normal if p > 0.05 can assume normal*

**Figure 6.51**

**Supporting Numerical and Graphical Evidence**

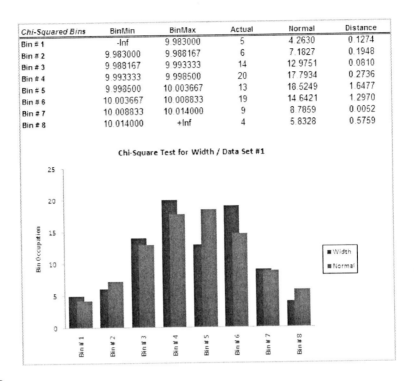

| Chi-Squared Bins | BinMin | BinMax | Actual | Normal | Distance |
|---|---|---|---|---|---|
| Bin # 1 | -Inf | 9.983000 | 5 | 4.2630 | 0.1274 |
| Bin # 2 | 9.983000 | 9.988167 | 6 | 7.1827 | 0.1948 |
| Bin # 3 | 9.988167 | 9.993333 | 14 | 12.9751 | 0.0810 |
| Bin # 4 | 9.993333 | 9.998500 | 20 | 17.7934 | 0.2736 |
| Bin # 5 | 9.998500 | 10.003667 | 13 | 18.5249 | 1.6477 |
| Bin # 6 | 10.003667 | 10.008833 | 19 | 14.6421 | 1.2970 |
| Bin # 7 | 10.008833 | 10.014000 | 9 | 8.7859 | 0.0052 |
| Bin # 8 | 10.014000 | +Inf | 4 | 5.8328 | 0.5759 |

Chi-Square Test for Width / Data Set #1

## Notes

- Any normality test, including the chi-square test, has difficulty distinguishing between normality and nonnormality unless the sample size is reasonably large—the larger, the better. On the other hand, with really large sample sizes, just about *anything* looks nonnormal, because any part of the histogram that is different from the corresponding normal histogram is "magnified" by the large sample size.

- The chi-square test has one drawback—its results can depend on the choice of bins for the histograms. Therefore, unless you have some special insights into any particular data set, it is probably best to accept the StatTools default bins.

# 6.3 Lilliefors Test

The **Lilliefors test** is a more powerful test for normality than the chi-square test. ("More powerful" means that it is more likely to detect nonnormality if it is present.) This procedure is based on a comparison of the **empirical cdf** and a normal cdf, where cdf stands for **cumulative distribution function**, the probability of being less than or equal to any particular value. The empirical cdf is based on the data. For example, if there are 100 observations and the 13th smallest is 137, then the empirical cdf, evaluated at 137, is 0.13. The Lilliefors test finds the maximum vertical distance between the empirical cdf and the normal cdf, and it compares this maximum to tabulated values that are based on sample size. If the observed maximum vertical distance is sufficiently large, this provides evidence that the data do *not* come from a normal distribution, so that the null hypothesis of normality can be rejected.

To run the Lilliefors test for the part width data, select **Lilliefors Test** from the **Normality Tests** dropdown and fill in the resulting dialog box as in Figure 6.6.

*Figure 6.6*

*Dialog Box for Lilliefors Test*

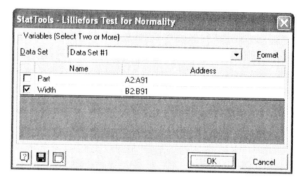

The output includes a graph of the empirical (staircase) and normal (smooth) cdfs shown in Figure 6.7 and the numeric data for the test in Figure 6.8. (StatTools also provides a table of data, not shown here, for building the graph.) If the data are normally distributed, there should be little vertical separation between the two curves in the graph. This is evidently the case with these data. Formally, the test statistic in Figure 6.8, 0.0513, is the maximum vertical separation between the two curves. The tabulated *critical* values (CVals) are shown below this test statistic for several significance levels. Because 0.0513 is less than each of these critical values, the normality hypothesis cannot be rejected at any of the usual significance levels. As with the chi-square test, this test indicates that a normality assumption for these data is quite plausible.

**Figure 6.7**

**Graphical Evidence from Lilliefors Test**

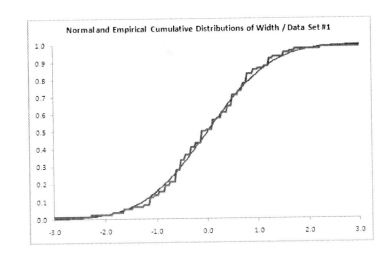

Normal and Empirical Cumulative Distributions of Width / Data Set #1

**Figure 6.8**

**Output for Hypothesis Test**

| Lilliefors Test Results | Width Data Set #1 |
|---|---|
| Sample Size | 90 |
| Sample Mean | 9.999256 |
| Sample Std Dev | 0.009728 |
| Test Statistic | 0.0513 |
| CVal (15% Sig. Level) | 0.0810 |
| CVal (10% Sig. Level) | 0.0856 |
| CVal (5% Sig. Level) | 0.0936 |
| CVal (2.5% Sig. Level) | 0.0998 |
| CVal (1% Sig. Level) | 0.1367 |

# 6.4 Q-Q Normal Plot

This final procedure creates a **quantile-quantile (Q-Q) plot** for a selected variable. It provides an informal test of normality. Although the details are somewhat involved, the objective is simple: to compare the quantiles (percentiles) for the data to the quantiles from a normal distribution. If the data are essentially normal, then the points on the Q-Q plot should be close to a 45-degree line. However, obvious curvature in the plot indicates some form of nonnormality, such as skewness.

To run the procedure, select **Q-Q Normal Plot** from the **Normality Tests** dropdown and fill in the resulting dialog box as in Figure 6.9. I suggest both of the bottom options. Unchecking the first option simply rescales the plot but does not affect its shape. The second option shows a 45-degree line for comparison.

*Figure 6.9*

*Dialog Box for Q-Q Normal Plot*

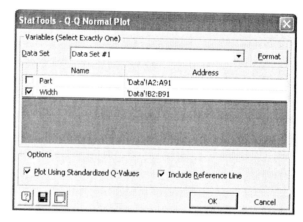

The Q-Q plot appears in Figure 6.10. You can now "eye-ball" the plot for obvious departures from a 45-degree line, such as curvature at either end. There is a hint of curvature in this plot, but it is not serious. Based on what you already know about this part width data set, it is not surprising that this Q-Q plot provides one more piece of evidence that the distribution of these data is reasonably normal.

*Figure 6.10*

*Q-Q Normal
Plot*

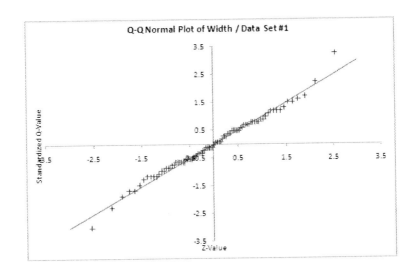

# Chapter 7: Data Utilities

## 7.1 Introduction

**Data
Utilities
Icon**

It is common in statistical analyses to begin with one data set and then transform it in some way before running various statistical procedures. You either transform existing variables or create entirely new variables from the original data. Excel is a particularly nice package for making such transformations. First, in most cases you can use formulas to link the new data to the original data. Second, you can place the new data wherever is most convenient: next to the original data set or on a new worksheet, say.

StatTools includes a number of utilities for transforming data to create new variables. Although all of these operations can be performed manually, and fairly easily, with standard Excel formulas, the StatTools utilities streamline the operations, and they avoid errors that might occur from entering the formulas manually.

Before introducing the various utilities, remember that one of the settings discussed in Chapter 2 is particularly important for the utilities in this chapter. By selecting the **Application Settings** from the **Utilities** dropdown, the dialog box in Figure 7.1 appears. The first setting in the Utilities group lets you select where to place newly created variables. The two options are to append the new variables to the current data set or to place them in a newly created data set. I almost always prefer the first option. This is because I typically create new variables to be used along with original variables in some statistical procedure, such as regression. Therefore, I want all of the original and new variables in a single data set. In this chapter, I use the first option unless stated otherwise.

*Figure 7.1*

*Application Settings*

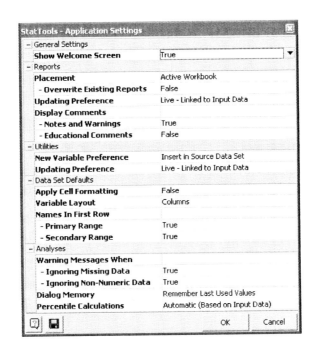

The second setting in the Utilities group lets you check whether you want the new variables to be "live" or static. If you check the "live" option, the new variables are linked to the original data through Excel formulas, so that if the original data change, the values of the new variables will change. I almost always prefer the "live" option.

# 7.2 Stacking and Unstacking Variables

The **stack** and **unstack** utilities are relevant when there is at least one *value* variable observed for each of several categories. For example, in the file **Empower Ratings.xlsx** used for illustration in this section, imagine that a company with five manufacturing plants in different regions of the country obtains a random sample of ratings of its new employee empowerment program. There is a sample from each plant, possibly with different sample sizes. If the data are in unstacked format, then there are five separate empowerment rating variables, one for each plant and possibly of different lengths. If the data are in stacked format, then there are two long variables, one identifying the plant and the other containing the ratings.

Data sets such as these are typically used in **comparison** problems, where the objective is to see whether there are differences in the distribution of ratings across the plants. All statistical software packages have a number of procedures for analyzing comparison problems. Most require that the data be in stacked format, although some allow the data to be unstacked. StatTools is capable of dealing with both formats, and its procedures allow you to choose which you have. Nevertheless, it is sometimes useful to convert from unstacked format to stacked format, or vice versa, and StatTools provides the utilities to do the conversion.

The data in Figure 7.2 illustrate the empowerment ratings for the plants in the various regions. These data are in unstacked format, with different variable lengths due to different sample sizes at the plants. To convert this data set to stacked format, select **Stack** from the **Data Utilities** dropdown and fill out the resulting dialog box as in Figure 7.3. You can check as many variables as you want to be stacked, although they should all be of the same measurement variable—in this case, empowerment rating. You then need to choose names for the categorical and measurement variables. I chose the names Plant and Rating.

**Figure 7.2**

**Data in Unstacked Format**

|  | A | B | C | D | E |
|---|---|---|---|---|---|
|  | South | Midwest | Northeast | Southwest | West |
| 1 | South | Midwest | Northeast | Southwest | West |
| 2 | 7 | 7 | 7 | 6 | 6 |
| 3 | 1 | 6 | 5 | 4 | 6 |
| 4 | 8 | 10 | 5 | 7 | 6 |
| 5 | 7 | 3 | 5 | 10 | 6 |
| 6 | 2 | 9 | 4 | 7 | 3 |
| 7 | 3 | 2 | 5 | 7 | 1 |
| 8 | 7 | 8 | 1 | 7 | 5 |
| 9 | 5 | 3 | 5 | 4 | 2 |
| 10 | 7 | 2 | 3 | 3 | 4 |
| 11 | 4 | 7 | 3 | 7 | 5 |
| 12 |  | 7 | 3 | 8 | 6 |
| 13 |  | 5 | 5 | 9 | 4 |
| 14 |  | 10 | 5 | 10 | 7 |
| 15 |  | 10 |  | 4 | 4 |
| 16 |  | 6 |  | 10 | 3 |
| 17 |  |  |  | 4 | 5 |
| 18 |  |  |  | 6 | 4 |
| 19 |  |  |  |  | 7 |
| 20 |  |  |  |  | 6 |
| 21 |  |  |  |  | 4 |

**Figure 7.3**

**Dialog Box for Stacking Variables**

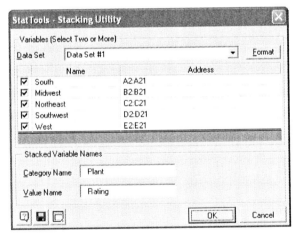

The resulting stacked data appear in Figure 7.4 (with many of the bottom rows not shown). Note that StatTools stacks the original variables on top of one another, using the original variable names for the categories in the Plant variable.

*Figure 7.4*

*Equivalent
Data in
Stacked
Format*

| | A | B |
|---|---|---|
| 1 | Plant | Rating |
| 2 | South | 7 |
| 3 | South | 1 |
| 4 | South | 8 |
| 5 | South | 7 |
| 6 | South | 2 |
| 7 | South | 3 |
| 8 | South | 7 |
| 9 | South | 5 |
| 10 | South | 7 |
| 11 | South | 4 |
| 12 | Midwest | 7 |
| 13 | Midwest | 6 |

It is possible to go the other way, unstacking the stacked data. To do so, starting from the data in Figure 7.4, select **Unstack** from the **Data Utilities** dropdown and fill in the resulting dialog box as in Figure 7.5. You need to select one variable (Plant) as the categorical variable and one (Rating) as the value variable.

*Figure 7.5*

*Dialog Box
for
Unstacking
Variables*

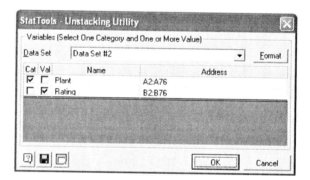

The resulting unstacked data appear in Figure 7.6. Except for the ordering of the variables and the variable names, this is the same data format we began with. Note how StatTools does this unstacking. It scans the categorical column selected in the dialog box for distinct values: Midwest, Northeast, and so on. For each distinct value, it creates a separate value variable in the unstacked format.

**Figure 7.6**

**Equivalent Data in Unstacked Format**

| | A | B | C | D | E |
|---|---|---|---|---|---|
| 1 | Rating(Midwest) | Rating(Northeast) | Rating(South) | Rating(Southwest) | Rating(West) |
| 2 | 7 | 7 | 7 | 6 | 6 |
| 3 | 6 | 5 | 1 | 4 | 6 |
| 4 | 10 | 5 | 8 | 7 | 6 |
| 5 | 3 | 5 | 7 | 10 | 6 |
| 6 | 9 | 4 | 2 | 7 | 3 |
| 7 | 2 | 5 | 3 | 7 | 1 |
| 8 | 8 | 1 | 7 | 7 | 5 |
| 9 | 3 | 5 | 5 | 4 | 2 |
| 10 | 2 | 3 | 7 | 3 | 4 |
| 11 | 7 | 3 | 4 | 7 | 5 |
| 12 | 7 | 3 | | 8 | 6 |
| 13 | 5 | 5 | | 9 | 4 |
| 14 | 10 | 5 | | 10 | 7 |
| 15 | 10 | | | 4 | 4 |
| 16 | 6 | | | 10 | 3 |
| 17 | | | | 4 | 5 |
| 18 | | | | 6 | 4 |
| 19 | | | | | 7 |
| 20 | | | | | 6 |
| 21 | | | | | 4 |

**Notes**

- This is one case where StatTools ignores the options checked in the Application Settings dialog box in Figure 7.1. It *always* puts the converted data in a new worksheet, and the new data are always static. This makes sense. It wouldn't be natural to append the converted data to the original data set, and it would be awkward at best to link the converted data to the original data through Excel formulas.

# 7.3 Transforming Variables

Many statistical analyses require variables to be related *linearly*. For this reason (and possibly others), it is often useful to transform one or more variables by some type of **nonlinear transformation**. StatTools implements four of the most common of these (natural logarithm, reciprocal, square, and square root), and it allows you to use your own custom functions for other transformations.

To illustrate these transformations, consider the data on family salaries and expenses in Figure 7.7. (This data set was used in Chapter 4. See the file **Expenses.xls** for the full data set.) If you plan to run a regression, say, of Salary versus the other variables (see Chapter 8), then it is conceivable that you might want to transform one or more of these variables. To do so, select **Transform** from the **Data Utilities** dropdown to obtain the dialog box in Figure 7.8. You can select one or more variables from the list and then apply the same transformation to each of them. From the Function dropdown list, you can select Log, Reciprocal, Square-Root, or Square, and you can also enter a "shift" constant other than the default value 0. Whatever you select appears in the Formula box. In this case, StatTools applies the STATLN function (the StatTools equivalent of Excel's LN natural logarithm function) to each value of each variable selected.

*Figure 7.7*

*Original Expense Variables*

|   | A | B | C | D |
|---|---|---|---|---|
| 1 | Salary | Culture | Sports | Dining |
| 2 | $54,600 | $1,020 | $990 | $1,510 |
| 3 | $57,500 | $1,100 | $460 | $1,180 |
| 4 | $53,300 | $900 | $780 | $1,590 |
| 5 | $43,500 | $570 | $860 | $1,750 |
| 6 | $57,200 | $900 | $1,390 | $2,120 |
| 7 | $63,400 | $820 | $1,880 | $3,090 |
| 8 | $58,500 | $1,340 | $710 | $1,540 |
| 9 | $55,600 | $1,250 | $680 | $1,800 |
| 10 | $61,300 | $1,190 | $1,220 | $2,330 |
| 11 | $61,100 | $640 | $1,480 | $2,670 |

**Figure 7.8**

**Dialog Box for Transforming Variables**

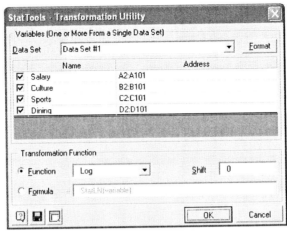

The transformed variables, appended to the original data set, appear in Figure 7.9. You could now use these log variables as part of a regression analysis or other procedure.

**Figure 7.9**

**Transformed Variables Appended to Original Variables**

| | A | B | C | D | E | F | G | H |
|---|---|---|---|---|---|---|---|---|
| 1 | Salary | Culture | Sports | Dining | Log(Salary) | Log(Culture) | Log(Sports) | Log(Dining) |
| 2 | $54,600 | $1,020 | $990 | $1,510 | 10.90778916 | 6.927557906 | 6.897704943 | 7.31986493 |
| 3 | $57,500 | $1,100 | $460 | $1,180 | 10.95954023 | 7.003065459 | 6.131226489 | 7.073269717 |
| 4 | $53,300 | $900 | $780 | $1,590 | 10.88369161 | 6.802394763 | 6.65929392 | 7.371489295 |
| 5 | $43,500 | $570 | $860 | $1,750 | 10.68051622 | 6.345636361 | 6.756932389 | 7.467371067 |
| 6 | $57,200 | $900 | $1,390 | $2,120 | 10.95430918 | 6.802394763 | 7.237059026 | 7.659171368 |
| 7 | $63,400 | $820 | $1,880 | $3,090 | 11.05721914 | 6.70930434 | 7.539027056 | 8.03592637 |
| 8 | $58,500 | $1,340 | $710 | $1,540 | 10.97678203 | 7.200424893 | 6.56526497 | 7.339537695 |
| 9 | $55,600 | $1,250 | $680 | $1,800 | 10.92593848 | 7.13089883 | 6.522092798 | 7.495541944 |
| 10 | $61,300 | $1,190 | $1,220 | $2,330 | 11.02353512 | 7.081708586 | 7.106606138 | 7.753623547 |

There are some transformations that result in errors. Specifically, you can't divide by 0, you can't take logarithms of nonpositive numbers (including 0), and you can't take square roots of negative numbers. Suppose you request the transformation in Figure 7.10. This transformation first subtracts 1000 from each value of Sports and then takes the square root. This results in an error for any value of Sports less than 1000. If you entered this formula manually into Excel, you would get results as shown in Figure 7.11—not good! This example simply illustrates that you have to be careful when transforming variables that your transformations are "legal."

**Figure 7.10**

**Asking for Logarithms of Negative Numbers**

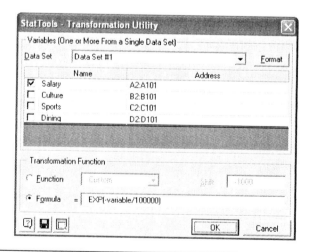

**Figure 7.11**

**Errors in Transformed Variables**

| | A | B | C | D | E |
|---|---|---|---|---|---|
| 1 | Salary | Culture | Sports | Dining | Sqt(Sports-1000) |
| 2 | $54,600 | $1,020 | $990 | $1,510 | #NUM! |
| 3 | $57,500 | $1,100 | $460 | $1,180 | #NUM! |
| 4 | $53,300 | $900 | $780 | $1,590 | #NUM! |
| 5 | $43,500 | $570 | $860 | $1,750 | #NUM! |
| 6 | $57,200 | $900 | $1,390 | $2,120 | 19.74841766 |
| 7 | $63,400 | $820 | $1,880 | $3,090 | 29.66479395 |

You can also enter your own custom formula for transforming variables. The dialog box in Figure 7.12 illustrates one possibility. Check the Formula option and enter the formula you want. This formula takes the negative of each value, divides by 100000, and takes EXP (the antilog function in Excel) of the result. The StatTools output appears in Figure 7.13. The variable name, which you might want to change, simply indicates that a custom function was used to transform Salary.

**Figure 7.12**

**Transforming with a Custom Function**

**Figure 7.13**

**Custom
Function
Results**

| | A | B | C | D | E |
|---|---|---|---|---|---|
| 1 | Salary | Culture | Sports | Dining | Func(Salary) |
| 2 | $54,600 | $1,020 | $990 | $1,510 | 0.579262231 |
| 3 | $57,500 | $1,100 | $460 | $1,180 | 0.562704869 |
| 4 | $53,300 | $900 | $780 | $1,590 | 0.586841801 |
| 5 | $43,500 | $570 | $860 | $1,750 | 0.647264667 |
| 6 | $57,200 | $900 | $1,390 | $2,120 | 0.564395518 |
| 7 | $63,400 | $820 | $1,880 | $3,090 | 0.530465689 |
| 8 | $58,500 | $1,340 | $710 | $1,540 | 0.557105862 |
| 9 | $55,600 | $1,250 | $680 | $1,800 | 0.573498476 |
| 10 | $61,300 | $1,190 | $1,220 | $2,330 | 0.541723259 |

## Notes

- If the variable to be transformed has missing values, StatTools treats the corresponding transformed values as missing.

# 7.4 Creating Dummy Variables

There are many times, particularly in regression analysis, where you need to incorporate a categorical variable in a quantitative analysis. This categorical variable might be a text variable, with values such as Male and Female, or it might be coded numerically, such as 1 for high school education only, 2 for undergraduate degree in college, or 3 for graduate degree in college. In either case, you should usually not use the categorical data in the form it is given. The trick is to create a **dummy variable** for each category, where the dummy variable equals 1 for each observation in the category and 0 for all other observations.

It is straightforward to create dummy variables with Excel IF functions. However, it is tedious. Therefore, StatTools automates the procedure. You first select a categorical variable. StatTools then scans this variable for distinct values and creates a dummy variable for each distinct value.

To illustrate, consider the data in Figure 7.14. (The full data set is in the file **Salaries 1.xlsx**.) Each employee is classified into one of three education levels, and the employee's gender is listed. StatTools can be used to create three dummy variables for education level and two for gender. To create the education level dummies, select **Dummy** from the **Data Utilities** dropdown and fill in the resulting dialog box as in Figure 7.15, checking the categorical variable EducLevel and choosing the first option in the bottom section. (I will discuss the second option shortly.)

*Figure 7.14*

*Salary Data*

| | A | B | C | D |
|---|---|---|---|---|
| 1 | Employee | EducLevel | Gender | Salary |
| 2 | 1 | 3 | Male | $32,000 |
| 3 | 2 | 1 | Female | $39,100 |
| 4 | 3 | 1 | Female | $33,200 |
| 5 | 4 | 2 | Female | $30,600 |
| 6 | 5 | 3 | Male | $29,000 |
| 7 | 6 | 3 | Female | $30,500 |
| 8 | 7 | 3 | Female | $30,000 |
| 9 | 8 | 3 | Male | $27,000 |
| 10 | 9 | 1 | Female | $34,000 |
| 11 | 10 | 3 | Female | $29,500 |

**Figure 7.15**

**Dialog Box for Dummy Variables from a Categorical Variable**

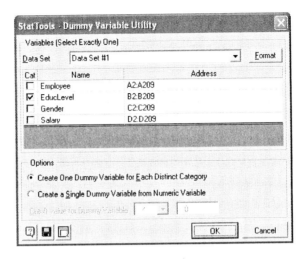

The resulting dummy variables, appended to the original data set, appear in Figure 7.16. Because there are three education levels, there are three dummies. Note that in each rows, exactly one of the dummies has value 1; the others have value 0.

**Figure 7.16**

**Data Set with Dummy Variables Appended**

| | A | B | C | D | E | F | G |
|---|---|---|---|---|---|---|---|
| 1 | Employee | EducLevel | Gender | Salary | EducLevel = 1 | EducLevel = 2 | EducLevel = 3 |
| 2 | 1 | 3 | Male | $32,000 | 0 | 0 | 1 |
| 3 | 2 | 1 | Female | $39,100 | 1 | 0 | 0 |
| 4 | 3 | 1 | Female | $33,200 | 1 | 0 | 0 |
| 5 | 4 | 2 | Female | $30,600 | 0 | 1 | 0 |
| 6 | 5 | 3 | Male | $29,000 | 0 | 0 | 1 |
| 7 | 6 | 3 | Female | $30,500 | 0 | 0 | 1 |
| 8 | 7 | 3 | Female | $30,000 | 0 | 0 | 1 |
| 9 | 8 | 3 | Male | $27,000 | 0 | 0 | 1 |
| 10 | 9 | 1 | Female | $34,000 | 1 | 0 | 0 |
| 11 | 10 | 3 | Female | $29,500 | 0 | 0 | 1 |

You can also create two dummies for the two possible genders. The procedure is exactly the same as for the education level dummies. In addition, you can create a dummy variable based on a *numeric* variable such as Salary. You first choose a condition on Salary, such as Salary < 30000, to specify whether the dummy is 1 or 0, and then fill in the dialog box as in Figure 7.17. Note that the dropdown list for the cutoff value can be any of the usual comparison operators: <, <=, =, >, >=, or <> (not equal). The resulting dummy based on salary appears in the right column of Figure 7.18.

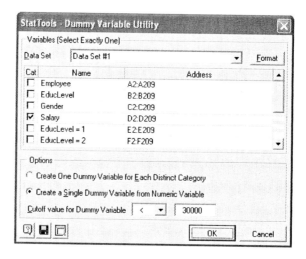

*Figure 7.17*

*Dialog Box for Dummy Variable from a Numeric Variable*

*Figure 7.18*

*Data Set with More Dummy Variables Appended*

| | A | B | C | D | E | F | G | H | I | J |
|---|---|---|---|---|---|---|---|---|---|---|
| 1 | Employee | EducLevel | Gender | Salary | EducLevel = 1 | EducLevel = 2 | EducLevel = 3 | Gender = Female | Gender = Male | Salary < 30000 |
| 2 | 1 | 3 | Male | $32,000 | 0 | 0 | 1 | 0 | 1 | 0 |
| 3 | 2 | 1 | Female | $39,100 | 1 | 0 | 0 | 1 | 0 | 0 |
| 4 | 3 | 1 | Female | $33,200 | 1 | 0 | 0 | 1 | 0 | 0 |
| 5 | 4 | 2 | Female | $30,600 | 0 | 1 | 0 | 1 | 0 | 0 |
| 6 | 5 | 3 | Male | $29,000 | 0 | 0 | 1 | 0 | 1 | 1 |
| 7 | 6 | 3 | Female | $30,500 | 0 | 0 | 1 | 1 | 0 | 0 |
| 8 | 7 | 3 | Female | $30,000 | 0 | 0 | 1 | 1 | 0 | 0 |
| 9 | 8 | 3 | Male | $27,000 | 0 | 0 | 1 | 0 | 1 | 1 |
| 10 | 9 | 1 | Female | $34,000 | 1 | 0 | 0 | 1 | 0 | 0 |
| 11 | 10 | 3 | Female | $29,500 | 0 | 0 | 1 | 1 | 0 | 1 |

**Notes**

- If the value of the categorical variable in some row is missing, StatTools treats the dummy values in this row as missing.

- If you (mistakenly) base a dummy on a numeric variable and choose the first option in the dummy variable dialog box, you will get a *lot* of dummy variables, one for each distinct value of the numeric variable. StatTools will warn you first before this happens.

# 7.5 Creating Interaction Variables

Interaction variables are, by definition, products of variables. The usual situation where you create interaction variables is for use in regression, discussed in Chapter 8. If you believe one variable X1 has an effect on some variable Y, but you believe this effect depends on the value of some other variable X2, then it makes sense to use the interaction variable X1*X2, the product of X1 and X2.

There are actually three types of interaction variables, depending on the nature of X1 and X2. If X1 and X2 are both numeric variables, then the interaction is simply their product. If X1 is numeric and X2 is categorical (even though it might be *coded* numerically), it makes sense to create the dummies for X2, perhaps named D21, D22, and D23 if there are three categories, and then create the three product variables X1*D21, X1*D22, and X1*D23—that is, you multiply the numeric variable by each of the dummies corresponding to the categorical variable. Finally, if X1 and X2 are both categorical, you proceed similarly, multiplying each of the dummies corresponding to X1 by each of the dummies corresponding to X2.

This is all straightforward, but it can be tedious, especially if there are more than two categories. However, StatTools does it easily. To illustrate, consider the data in Figure 7.19. (See the full data set in the file **Salaries 2.xlsx**.) If Salary is the variable you are trying to explain, it is conceivable that there could be (1) an interaction between the numeric variables Age and YrsExper, (2) an interaction between the numeric variable YrsExper and the categorical variable Gender, and/or (3) an interaction between the categorical variables Gender and EducLevel.

*Figure 7.19*

*Salary Data*

| | A | B | C | D | E | F |
|---|---|---|---|---|---|---|
| 1 | Employee | Age | Gender | EducLevel | YrsExper | Salary |
| 2 | 1 | 26 | Male | 3 | 3 | 32000 |
| 3 | 2 | 38 | Female | 1 | 14 | 39100 |
| 4 | 3 | 35 | Female | 1 | 12 | 33200 |
| 5 | 4 | 40 | Female | 2 | 8 | 30600 |
| 6 | 5 | 28 | Male | 3 | 3 | 29000 |
| 7 | 6 | 24 | Female | 3 | 3 | 30500 |
| 8 | 7 | 27 | Female | 3 | 4 | 30000 |
| 9 | 8 | 33 | Male | 3 | 8 | 27000 |
| 10 | 9 | 62 | Female | 1 | 4 | 34000 |
| 11 | 10 | 31 | Female | 3 | 9 | 29500 |

To create these interaction variables, select **Interaction** from the **Data Utilities** dropdown. This brings up the dialog box in Figure 7.20. The key is the dropdown list at the top, shown here in expanded form. If you choose the first item in the list, StatTools asks you to select two numeric variables (as shown here). If you select the second item, it asks you to select a numeric and a categorical variable. If you choose the third item, it asks you to select two categorical variables.

*Figure 7.20*

*Dialog Box
for
Interactions*

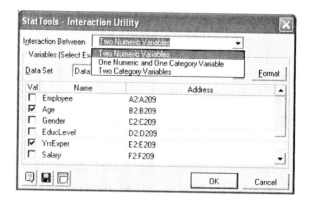

After creating all three types of interactions discussed above, the output appears as in Figure 7.21. (I have changed the default names StatTools gives to these variables to make the output fit on the page.) The IA1 variable is the product of Age and YrsExper. The IA2_1 and IA2_2 variables are the products of YrsExper and the two dummies for Gender. The last six interaction variables are the products of the two dummies for Gender and the three dummies for EducLevel. (This explains why they are all 0's and 1's.) Keep in mind that these interaction variables are usually meaningless on their own, but they allow you to model various relationships in regression analyses.

*Figure 7.21*

*Interaction
Between
Variables*

| | G | H | I | J | K | L | M | N | O |
|---|---|---|---|---|---|---|---|---|---|
| 1 | IA1 | IA2_1 | IA2_2 | IA3_1 | IA3_2 | IA3_3 | IA3_4 | IA3_5 | IA3_6 |
| 2 | 78 | 0 | 3 | 0 | 0 | 0 | 0 | 0 | 1 |
| 3 | 532 | 14 | 0 | 1 | 0 | 0 | 0 | 0 | 0 |
| 4 | 420 | 12 | 0 | 1 | 0 | 0 | 0 | 0 | 0 |
| 5 | 320 | 8 | 0 | 0 | 1 | 0 | 0 | 0 | 0 |
| 6 | 84 | 0 | 3 | 0 | 0 | 0 | 0 | 0 | 0 |
| 7 | 72 | 3 | 0 | 0 | 0 | 1 | 0 | 0 | 1 |
| 8 | 108 | 4 | 0 | 0 | 0 | 1 | 0 | 0 | 0 |
| 9 | 264 | 0 | 8 | 0 | 0 | 0 | 0 | 0 | 1 |
| 10 | 248 | 4 | 0 | 1 | 0 | 0 | 0 | 0 | 0 |

# 7.6 Creating Combination Variables

It is occasionally useful to combine variables in different ways. StatTools implements several types of combinations, including the product, the sum, the average, the minimum, the maximum, and the range (maximum minus minimum). It performs these operations row by row for the variables you select.

A good example of a data set where these operations make sense appears in Figure 7.22. (See the file **Test Scores.xlsx**.) Each student takes four tests, with the scores shown. You can use the StatTools combination utility to summarize the scores for each student in various ways. To do so, select **Combination** from the **Data Utilities** dropdown. In the resulting dialog box, shown in Figure 7.23, you can select any number of variables and a combination type.

*Figure 7.22*

*Test Score Data*

| | A | B | C | D | E |
|---|---|---|---|---|---|
| 1 | Student | Test1 | Test2 | Test3 | Test4 |
| 2 | 1 | 62 | 68 | 79 | 76 |
| 3 | 2 | 85 | 75 | 75 | 75 |
| 4 | 3 | 90 | 75 | 83 | 91 |
| 5 | 4 | 66 | 63 | 64 | 71 |
| 6 | 5 | 77 | 75 | 68 | 70 |
| 7 | 6 | 69 | 60 | 65 | 67 |
| 8 | 7 | 70 | 83 | 83 | 77 |
| 9 | 8 | 73 | 81 | 72 | 65 |
| 10 | 9 | 64 | 58 | 52 | 56 |

*Figure 7.23*

*Dialog Box for Combinations*

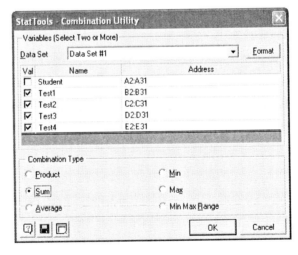

I ran this separately for the Sum, Average, Min, Max, and Range combinations, with the results shown in Figure 7.24. (I shortened the StatTools default variable names to make the output fit on the page.) Note that I could also have chosen the Product option, but it doesn't make much sense in this context.

Figure 7.24

Combinations
of Variables

| | A | B | C | D | E | F | G | H | I |
|---|---|---|---|---|---|---|---|---|---|
| 1 | Student | Test1 | Test2 | Test3 | Test4 | Sum | Min | Max | Range |
| 2 | 1 | 62 | 68 | 79 | 76 | 285 | 62 | 79 | 17 |
| 3 | 2 | 85 | 75 | 75 | 75 | 310 | 75 | 85 | 10 |
| 4 | 3 | 90 | 75 | 83 | 91 | 339 | 75 | 91 | 16 |
| 5 | 4 | 66 | 63 | 64 | 71 | 264 | 63 | 71 | 8 |
| 6 | 5 | 77 | 75 | 68 | 70 | 290 | 68 | 77 | 9 |
| 7 | 6 | 69 | 60 | 65 | 67 | 261 | 60 | 69 | 9 |
| 8 | 7 | 70 | 83 | 83 | 77 | 313 | 70 | 83 | 13 |
| 9 | 8 | 73 | 81 | 72 | 65 | 291 | 65 | 81 | 16 |
| 10 | 9 | 64 | 58 | 52 | 56 | 230 | 52 | 64 | 12 |

# 7.7 Creating Lagged Variables and Difference Variables

In time series analysis, it is often useful to create lagged and/or difference variables corresponding to a time series variable. A **lagged variable** for a given **lag** shows previous values of the variable. For example, with monthly data, the lag 1 variable corresponding to the March observation is the February observation, and the lag 2 variable corresponding to the March observation is the January observation. To create a lagged variable for a given lag in Excel, StatTools essentially "pushes down" the variable by the number of rows specified by the lag.

In contrast, a **difference variable** takes differences between adjacent observations. The first difference takes differences between successive values of the original variable. This is the most common difference variable used in time series analysis. However, it is sometimes useful to analyze the second difference, defined as the difference between successive values of the first difference variable. It is even possible to create third differences, fourth differences, and so on, but these are rarely useful.

To understand lagged and difference variables, consider the sales data in Figure 7.25. (The full data set is in the file **Stereo Sales.xlsx**.) To create the first two lagged variables, select **Lag** from the **Data Utilities** dropdown and fill in the resulting dialog box as in Figure 7.26. You can request any number of lags, but a small number is usually sufficient. StatTools then creates a lagged variable for each of the lags requested, as shown in Figure 7.27. Note that there are missing values at the beginning of the lagged series. For example, the lag 1 for Jan-05 is missing because it corresponds to the missing Dec-04 observation.

*Figure 7.25*

*Stereo Sales Data*

|    | A      | B     |
|----|--------|-------|
| 1  | Month  | Sales |
| 2  | Jan-05 | 226   |
| 3  | Feb-05 | 254   |
| 4  | Mar-05 | 204   |
| 5  | Apr-05 | 193   |
| 6  | May-05 | 191   |
| 7  | Jun-05 | 166   |
| 8  | Jul-05 | 175   |
| 9  | Aug-05 | 217   |
| 10 | Sep-05 | 167   |
| 11 | Oct-05 | 192   |

*Figure 7.26*

*Dialog Box
for Lagged
Variables*

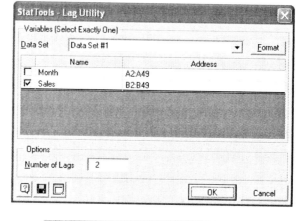

*Figure 7.27*

*Lagged
Variables
Appended
to Original
Variable*

|    | A | B | C | D |
|----|---|---|---|---|
| 1 | Month | Sales | Lag1(Sales) | Lag2(Sales) |
| 2 | Jan-05 | 226 | | |
| 3 | Feb-05 | 254 | 226 | |
| 4 | Mar-05 | 204 | 254 | 226 |
| 5 | Apr-05 | 193 | 204 | 254 |
| 6 | May-05 | 191 | 193 | 204 |
| 7 | Jun-05 | 166 | 191 | 193 |
| 8 | Jul-05 | 175 | 166 | 191 |
| 9 | Aug-05 | 217 | 175 | 166 |
| 10 | Sep-05 | 167 | 217 | 175 |
| 11 | Oct-05 | 192 | 167 | 217 |
| 12 | Nov-05 | 127 | 192 | 167 |
| 13 | Dec-05 | 148 | 127 | 192 |

The procedure for creating difference variables is similar. For example, to create the first two difference variables, select **Difference** from the **Data Utilities** dropdown and fill in the resulting dialog box as in Figure 7.28. This creates the two difference variables in Figure 7.29. Again, there are missing values at the beginning of the difference series. For example, the first difference corresponding Jan-05 is the Jan-05 value minus the Dec-04 value, and the latter is missing.

*Figure 7.28*

*Dialog Box
for
Difference
Variables*

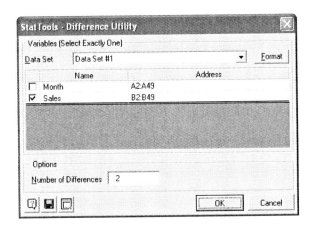

*Figure 7.29*

*Difference
Variables
Appended
to Original
Variable*

|   | A | B | C | D |
|---|------|-------|-------------|-------------|
| 1 | Month | Sales | Diff1(Sales) | Diff2(Sales) |
| 2 | Jan-05 | 226 | | |
| 3 | Feb-05 | 254 | 28 | |
| 4 | Mar-05 | 204 | -50 | -78 |
| 5 | Apr-05 | 193 | -11 | 39 |
| 6 | May-05 | 191 | -2 | 9 |
| 7 | Jun-05 | 166 | -25 | -23 |
| 8 | Jul-05 | 175 | 9 | 34 |
| 9 | Aug-05 | 217 | 42 | 33 |
| 10 | Sep-05 | 167 | -50 | -92 |
| 11 | Oct-05 | 192 | 25 | 75 |
| 12 | Nov-05 | 127 | -65 | -90 |
| 13 | Dec-05 | 148 | 21 | 86 |

**Notes**

- For the lagged variable and difference variable procedures, StatTools allows missing values anywhere in the series.

# 7.8 Generating Random Samples

It is occasionally useful to generate random samples from a larger data set and record their values. StatTools performs this operation easily. Consider the data set from Section 7.4 on employee salaries. (See the full data set in the file **Salaries 1.xlsx**. It has data on 208 employees.) To generate several random samples of a given sample size from this data set, select **Random Sample** from the **Data Utilities** dropdown. The resulting dialog box in Figure 7.30 gives you several choices. First, you can select any or all of the variables to be included. (I omitted EducLevel for illustration only.) Next, you must specify the number of samples and the sample size. I chose 3 samples of size 10 each.

*Figure 7.30*

*Dialog Box for Generating Random Samples*

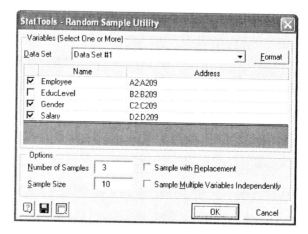

Finally, you can check any of three optional boxes. If you check the Sample with Replacement option, then the *same* employee can appear more than once in the same sample. I left it unchecked, so that each sample will consist of distinct employees. If you check the Sample Multiple Variables Independently, then the resulting rows will be mixed up. For example, if 1 is selected from the Employee variable, the gender and salary in the resulting row of the sample will probably *not* be the gender and salary of employee 1. This option should be checked only in rare circumstances. You usually want to keep whole rows intact. If you check the Include Blanks in Sample, then it is possible that rows with missing data will be included in the samples.

The results appear in Figure 7.31. Note that StatTools creates a single data set for the 3 samples, with the variables labeled consecutively. Also, note that if you run this procedure again, with exactly the same dialog settings, you will obtain *different* random samples. This is due to the random numbers StatTools uses to generate these samples.

*Figure 7.31*

*Random Samples*

| | A | B | C | D | E | F | G | H | I |
|---|---|---|---|---|---|---|---|---|---|
| 1 | Employee(1) | Gender(1) | Salary(1) | Employee(2) | Gender(2) | Salary(2) | Employee(3) | Gender(3) | Salary(3) |
| 2 | 43 | Female | 33500 | 4 | Female | 30600 | 135 | Male | 39500 |
| 3 | 101 | Female | 35300 | 107 | Female | 36200 | 203 | Male | 74000 |
| 4 | 56 | Female | 29800 | 87 | Female | 31900 | 122 | Male | 36300 |
| 5 | 141 | Female | 39700 | 160 | Male | 45500 | 127 | Female | 37000 |
| 6 | 154 | Male | 42500 | 68 | Female | 41400 | 188 | Female | 61800 |
| 7 | 40 | Male | 30500 | 35 | Female | 34300 | 84 | Male | 34920 |
| 8 | 133 | Female | 35300 | 162 | Female | 44000 | 100 | Female | 38000 |
| 9 | 12 | Female | 31300 | 11 | Female | 26800 | 151 | Female | 40260 |
| 10 | 174 | Male | 47500 | 49 | Female | 34000 | 6 | Female | 30500 |
| 11 | 19 | Female | 32600 | 131 | Female | 43600 | 8 | Male | 27000 |

# Chapter 8: Regression and Classification

## 8.1 Introduction

*Regression and Classification Icon*

An important part of statistical analysis involves building models that relate one variable to other variables. StatTools provides the most popular procedures for doing this. It implements several versions of regression analysis, arguably the most important "advanced" technique in the analyst's arsenal. It also implements logistic regression and discriminant analysis, two procedures for classifying observations into two or more categories, given values of related variables. These latter two methods are often considered advanced "multivariate" statistical methods and are not always available in statistical software packages. However, they are becoming increasingly important for real business problems, as well as for problems in other areas.

## 8.2 Regression

Regression is one of the most frequently used statistical techniques, both because of its power and its flexibility. It allows you to "explain" a variable such as salary from values of other related variables. The variable to be explained is called the **dependent variable** and is often labeled Y. The variables used to explain Y are called the **independent variables** (or **explanatory variables**) and are often labeled X's. The objective is to estimate a **regression equation** for Y in terms of the X's, using the method of **least squares**. The resulting equation serves two purposes. First, by examining the coefficients of the X's, you can better understand "how the world works." For example, you can better understand the salary structure in a company or housing prices in a community. Second, the regression equation allows you to predict new values of Y, given the corresponding values of the X's.

Analysts often distinguish between **simple regression**, which allows only a single X in the equation, and **multiple regression**, which allows any number of X's in the equation. StatTools does not make this distinction. Its multiple regression procedure allows one or more X's to be selected. Virtually all statistical software packages include multiple regression, and StatTools is no exception. However, unlike some packages, StatTools also provides a set of procedures for building a regression equation step by step, as many analysts prefer to do. These include the "true" **stepwise** procedure, a **forward** stepwise procedure, and a **backward** stepwise procedure. It even includes a somewhat nonstandard **block** procedure. All of these are discussed in this chapter.

**Multiple Regression**

To run a multiple regression analysis, you must specify a Y variable and one or more related X variables. StatTools then estimates an equation that relates Y linearly to the X's. It estimates this equation with the standard **least squares** method. For each observation, it substitutes the X's into any proposed equation to obtain a **fitted** (or predicted) value of Y. The difference between the actual Y and the fitted Y is called a **residual**. The least squares method finds the equation that minimizes the sum of squared residuals, where the sum is over all observations. StatTools provides a list of the fitted values and residuals, along with a number of scatterplots involving these variables, so that you can better understand the results and detect any suspicious behavior, such as outliers.

The X's for any multiple regression analysis can be original variables, or they can include new variables created from the original variables, possibly with the StatTools data utilities discussed in the previous chapter. To illustrate, consider the salary data in Figure 8.1. (See the full data set in the file **Salaries 3.xlsx**.) This data set includes the character variable Gender, a numerically coded categorical variable EducLevel, and a numeric variable YrsExper, all of which could be related to the dependent variable Salary. To explain salary with this data set, you would almost surely create several new variables first, as shown in Figure 8.2. These include a dummy variable for females, an interaction variable between the Female dummy and YrsExper (to allow the effect of YrsExper on Salary to depend on gender), and dummies for the three education levels. Once you create any extra variables you think you might need, you are then ready to run one or more regressions.

**Figure 8.1**

**Salary Data**

| | A | B | C | D | E | F |
|---|---|---|---|---|---|---|
| 1 | Employee | Age | Gender | EducLevel | YrsExper | Salary |
| 2 | 1 | 26 | Male | 3 | 3 | 32000 |
| 3 | 2 | 38 | Female | 1 | 14 | 39100 |
| 4 | 3 | 35 | Female | 1 | 12 | 33200 |
| 5 | 4 | 40 | Female | 2 | 8 | 30600 |
| 6 | 5 | 28 | Male | 3 | 3 | 29000 |
| 7 | 6 | 24 | Female | 3 | 3 | 30500 |
| 8 | 7 | 27 | Female | 3 | 4 | 30000 |
| 9 | 8 | 33 | Male | 3 | 8 | 27000 |
| 10 | 9 | 62 | Female | 1 | 4 | 34000 |
| 11 | 10 | 31 | Female | 3 | 9 | 29500 |

**Figure 8.2**

**Salary Data with Extra Variables**

| | A | B | C | D | E | F | G | H | I | J | K |
|---|---|---|---|---|---|---|---|---|---|---|---|
| 1 | Employee | Age | Gender | EducLevel | YrsExper | Salary | Female | Female*YrsExper | EducLevel1 | EducLevel2 | EducLevel3 |
| 2 | 1 | 26 | Male | 3 | 3 | 32000 | 0 | 0 | 0 | 0 | 1 |
| 3 | 2 | 38 | Female | 1 | 14 | 39100 | 1 | 14 | 1 | 0 | 0 |
| 4 | 3 | 35 | Female | 1 | 12 | 33200 | 1 | 12 | 1 | 0 | 0 |
| 5 | 4 | 40 | Female | 2 | 8 | 30600 | 1 | 8 | 0 | 1 | 0 |
| 6 | 5 | 28 | Male | 3 | 3 | 29000 | 0 | 0 | 0 | 0 | 1 |
| 7 | 6 | 24 | Female | 3 | 3 | 30500 | 1 | 3 | 0 | 0 | 1 |
| 8 | 7 | 27 | Female | 3 | 4 | 30000 | 1 | 4 | 0 | 0 | 1 |
| 9 | 8 | 33 | Male | 3 | 8 | 27000 | 0 | 0 | 0 | 0 | 1 |
| 10 | 9 | 62 | Female | 1 | 4 | 34000 | 1 | 4 | 1 | 0 | 0 |
| 11 | 10 | 31 | Female | 3 | 9 | 29500 | 1 | 9 | 0 | 0 | 1 |

To run a multiple regression, select **Regression** from the **Regression &**
**Classification** dropdown and fill in the resulting dialog box as in Figure 8.3. From
the top dropdown list you can select Multiple or any of the stepwise options
discussed shortly. Then you must select at least one independent (I) variable (I
have selected only two, Age and YrsExper) and exactly one dependent (D) variable.
The bottom section provides a number of optional graphs for diagnostic purposes. I
have selected the most common diagnostic graph, of residuals versus fitted values,
but you can select as many as you like or none. You can also check the Include
Prediction option, which I will explain shortly.

*Figure 8.3*

*Dialog Box*
*for*
*Regression*

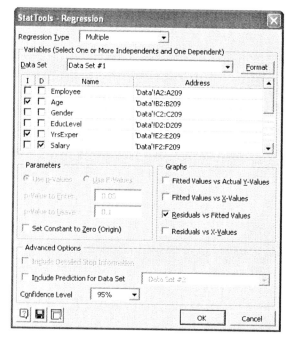

For the options requested in Figure 8.3, the StatTools output consists of three parts:
(1) the basic regression output in Figure 8.4, the list of fitted values and residuals in
Figure 8.5, and the scatterplot of residuals versus fitted values in Figure 8.6. The
output in Figure 8.4 is similar to regression output from all statistical packages. The
top section lists summary measures from the regression, the middle section
provides a test for whether the independent variables, as a whole, explain a
significant percentage of variation in Salary, and the bottom section provides
information about the regression equation, including 95% confidence intervals for
the regression coefficients. When Age and YrsExper are the only explanatory
variables, the output indicates that (1) 38.2% of the variation in salary is explained
(R-square), (2) a ballpark estimate of the prediction errors made from using the
equation is $8895 (the standard error of estimate), (3) each extra year of experience
is expected to contribute about $1069 to salary, and (4) the negative coefficient of
Age is insignificant (high p-value).

---

*Figure 8.4*

*Basic
Regression
Output*

| Summary | Multiple R | R-Square | Adjusted R-Square | StErr of Estimate | | |
|---|---|---|---|---|---|---|
| | 0.6177 | 0.3816 | 0.3756 | 8894.724 | | |

| ANOVA Table | Degrees of Freedom | Sum of Squares | Mean of Squares | F-Ratio | p-Value | |
|---|---|---|---|---|---|---|
| Explained | 2 | 10008305330 | 5004152665 | 63.2507 | < 0.0001 | |
| Unexplained | 205 | 16218801900 | 79116106.83 | | | |

| Regression Table | Coefficient | Standard Error | t-Value | p-Value | Confidence Interval 95% Lower | Upper |
|---|---|---|---|---|---|---|
| Constant | 32676.547 | 2727.641 | 11.9798 | < 0.0001 | 27298.721 | 38054.372 |
| Age | -76.639 | 82.145 | -0.9330 | 0.3519 | -238.596 | 85.318 |
| YrsExper | 1069.066 | 121.304 | 8.8131 | < 0.0001 | 829.903 | 1308.230 |

The fitted values and residuals in Figure 8.5 are the basis for the scatterplot in Figure 8.6. This scatterplot allows you to look for any suspicious patterns or points. In this case, several of the points at the right on the graph have suspiciously large residuals (4 positive and 1 negative). You might want to examine these particular employees more closely to see why they fall outside the general pattern.

*Figure 8.5*

*Fitted
Values and
Residuals*

| Graph Data | Salary | Fit | Residual |
|---|---|---|---|
| 1 | 32000 | 33891.12438 | -1891.124383 |
| 2 | 39100 | 44731.1833 | -5631.183299 |
| 3 | 33200 | 42822.96837 | -9622.96837 |
| 4 | 30600 | 38163.50632 | -7563.50632 |
| 5 | 29000 | 33737.8458 | -4737.845803 |
| 6 | 30500 | 34044.40296 | -3544.402963 |
| 7 | 30000 | 34883.55149 | -4883.551493 |
| 8 | 27000 | 38699.98135 | -11699.98135 |
| 9 | 34000 | 32201.17634 | 1798.823661 |
| 10 | 29500 | 39922.32633 | -10422.32633 |

*Figure 8.6*

*Scatterplot
of
Residuals
Versus
Fitted
Values*

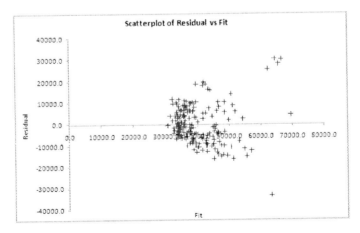

The fitted values and residuals in Figure 8.5 are the basis

StatTools provides an interface for making predictions for new observations. Although there is some flexibility on how this can be used, I recommend the following setup. In some unused section of the data worksheet, probably either below the original data set or to the right of it, copy the variable names and enter the values of the X's for the new observations, as in Figure 8.7. However, you do *not* need to enter the values of Y (salary in this case) for these observations. Indeed, this is the whole purpose of the prediction—to predict unknown Y's from given X's. Then use the StatTools data set manager to define this as a new data set (mine is called Data Set #2) and run the regression again, this time checking the **Include Prediction** option and selecting Data Set #2 as the prediction data set in the regression dialog box (see Figure 8.8).

*Figure 8.7*

*Data Set for Prediction*

| | M | N | O | P | Q | R | S | T | U | V | W |
|---|---|---|---|---|---|---|---|---|---|---|---|
| 1 | Employee | Age | Gender | EducLevel | YrsExper | Salary | Female | Female*YrsExper | EducLevel1 | EducLevel2 | EducLevel3 |
| 2 | 209 | 37 | Female | 3 | 7 | | 1 | 7 | 0 | 0 | 1 |
| 3 | 210 | 49 | Male | 2 | 10 | | 0 | 0 | 0 | 1 | 0 |
| 4 | 211 | 55 | Male | 3 | 16 | | 0 | 0 | 0 | 0 | 1 |

*Figure 8.81*

*Section of Regression Dialog Box with Prediction Option*

Advanced Options

☐ Include Detailed Step Information

☑ Include Prediction   Data Set   [ Data Set #2 ▼ ]

StatTools substitutes the given values of the X's into the regression equation to obtain predictions of the Y's. It also calculates 95% prediction intervals for these predictions. In fact, if there are no Lower Limit and Upper Limit columns in your prediction data set for the prediction intervals, it asks you whether you want these to be added, as in Figure 8.9. You should click on Yes. The resulting predictions and prediction intervals appear in Figure 8.10.

*Figure 8.9*

*Prediction Interval Message*

StatTools

Matching variable not found in prediction data set for lower limit variable. Do you want to insert new variable in Data Set?

[ Yes ]      [ No ]

*Figure 8.10*

*Prediction Output*

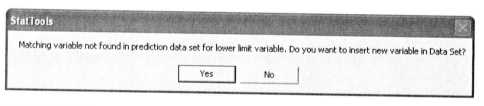

| | M | N | O | P | Q | R | S | T | U | V | W | X | Y |
|---|---|---|---|---|---|---|---|---|---|---|---|---|---|
| 1 | Employee | Age | Gender | EducLevel | YrsExper | Salary | Female | Female*YrsExper | EducLevel1 | EducLevel2 | EducLevel3 | LowerLimit95 | UpperLimit95 |
| 2 | 209 | 37 | Female | 3 | 7 | 37324 | 1 | 7 | 0 | 0 | 1 | 19736.84291 | 54909.87267 |
| 3 | 210 | 49 | Male | 2 | 10 | 39612 | 0 | 0 | 0 | 1 | 0 | 21981.80066 | 57241.97036 |
| 4 | 211 | 55 | Male | 3 | 16 | 45566 | 0 | 0 | 0 | 0 | 1 | 27902.70306 | 63230.19327 |

StatTools makes it easy to run several regressions on the same data set. It remembers your previous choices in the regression dialog box so that only minor modifications are necessary on subsequent runs. I illustrate one further regression run with the salary data, using the dummies and interaction variable mentioned earlier. All you need to do is check the extra variables shown in Figure 8.11. For illustration, I have deliberately chosen all three dummies corresponding to the EducLevel categorical variable. This is something you should *not* do in regression because it creates an exact linear relationship among the X's. StatTools checks for this and issues the warning in Figure 8.12. This warning prompts you to get rid of one of the dummies. I chose to uncheck the dummy for education level 1. It then becomes the **reference category**, to which the other categories can be compared.

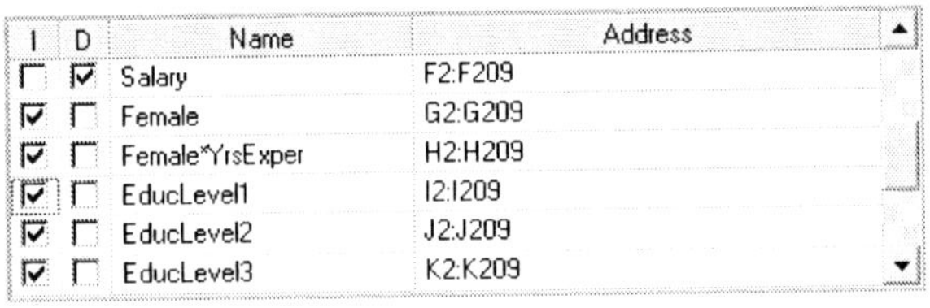

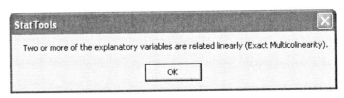

*Figure 8.11*

*Selection of Too Many Dummy Variables*

*Figure 8.12*

*Warning of Exact Linear Relationship*

The resulting regression output appears in Figure 8.13. It is significantly better than the equation with only Age and YrsExper. For example, R-square is up to 69.4% and the standard error of estimate is down to $6320. In addition, all of the included variables are significant (low p-values) except for Age and the dummy corresponding to education level 2. Evidently, Age is not important and education levels 1 and 2 could be combined to get a somewhat more parsimonious equation. (**Parsimony** means explaining the most with the least. It is always good to strive for parsimony when building regression models.)

The coefficients of YrsExper, Female, and Female*YrsExper require some interpretation. For males, the latter two variables can be ignored (because the variable Female equals 0 for males), so males can be expected to get $1446 more in salary for each extra year of experience. For females, the coefficient of Female means that they are expected to start with a $4485 bonus over males, but the negative coefficient of the interaction variable means that their increase in salary for every extra year of experience is $1097 less than for males. In other words, females start higher but go up at a much slower rate.

**Figure 8.13**

**Regression
Output with
Dummies
and
Interaction**

| Summary | Multiple R | R-Square | Adjusted R-Square | StErr of Estimate | | |
|---|---|---|---|---|---|---|
| | 0.8330 | 0.6939 | 0.6847 | 6320.295 | | |

| ANOVA Table | Degrees of Freedom | Sum of Squares | Mean of Squares | F-Ratio | p-Value | |
|---|---|---|---|---|---|---|
| Explained | 6 | 18197935168 | 3032989195 | 75.9270 | < 0.0001 | |
| Unexplained | 201 | 8029172063 | 39946129.67 | | | |

| Regression Table | Coefficient | Standard Error | t-Value | p-Value | Confidence Interval 95% | |
|---|---|---|---|---|---|---|
| | | | | | Lower | Upper |
| Constant | 22820.405 | 2639.847 | 8.6446 | < 0.0001 | 17615.058 | 28025.752 |
| Age | 69.382 | 61.507 | 1.1280 | 0.2606 | -51.899 | 190.664 |
| YrsExper | 1446.309 | 106.001 | 13.6443 | < 0.0001 | 1237.292 | 1655.325 |
| Female | 4484.979 | 1552.457 | 2.8890 | 0.0043 | 1423.788 | 7546.169 |
| Female*YrsExper | -1097.400 | 129.358 | -8.4834 | < 0.0001 | -1352.473 | -842.326 |
| EducLevel2 | 517.326 | 1510.205 | 0.3426 | 0.7323 | -2460.552 | 3495.204 |
| EducLevel3 | 6494.918 | 1302.633 | 4.9860 | < 0.0001 | 3926.339 | 9063.496 |

## Stepwise Regression Procedures

With the StatTools multiple regression procedure, you select a Y and a set of X's, and StatTools estimates the equation with all of these X's included — regardless of whether they are significant. Many analysts prefer to use a stepwise method instead, especially when there are many potential X's that might be related to Y. StatTools implements three traditional stepwise procedures.

The **forward** method starts with no X's and at each step adds the variable that explains the most of the variance of Y still left unexplained by the X's already in the equation. If none of the X's not yet in the equation are significant, the procedure quits, with these X's left out of the final equation. The **backward** method begins with all of the selected X's in the equation and at each step deletes the variable that is least significant. If all remaining variables are significant, the procedure quits. The true **stepwise** method is almost the same as the forward method, but it has the option of deleting a previously entered variable if this variable becomes insignificant. For all of these methods, you can specify the significance levels for entering or leaving, either as p-values (preferred for simplicity) or the corresponding F values.

To illustrate these stepwise methods, consider the sales data in Figure 8.14 for a company that sells its products through mail-order catalogs. (The full data set is in the file **Catalog Spending.xlsx**.) The key variable here is AmountSpent, the amount the customer spent this year with the company. There are many potential explanatory variables, including demographic data (Gender is 1 for males, Own Home is 1 for homeowners, Married is 1 for married people, and Close is 1 for people who live reasonably close to shopping centers), data about previous spending with the company, and the number of catalogs sent to the customer this year. You could build an equation for AmountSpent that includes all of these variables, but it makes sense to use a stepwise method to identify the significant variables. To do so, select **Regression** from the **Regression & Classification** dropdown. The top dropdown list in the resulting dialog box appears in Figure

8.15. For now, select the Stepwise option, select all variables other than Customer as potential X's, choose the default p-values (0.05 to enter, 0.1 to leave), and check the option to Include Detailed Step Information.

**Figure 8.14**

**Catalog Spending Data**

| | A | B | C | D | E | F | G | H | I | J | K | L |
|---|---|---|---|---|---|---|---|---|---|---|---|---|
| 1 | Customer | Age | Gender | Own Home | Married | Close | Salary | Children | PrevCust | PrevSpent | Catalogs | AmountSpent |
| 2 | 1 | 73 | 0 | 0 | 0 | 1 | $16,400 | 1 | 1 | $246 | 12 | $218 |
| 3 | 2 | 22 | 0 | 1 | 1 | 0 | $108,100 | 3 | 1 | $1,622 | 18 | $2,632 |
| 4 | 3 | 51 | 1 | 1 | 1 | 1 | $97,300 | 1 | 0 | $0 | 12 | $3,048 |
| 5 | 4 | 48 | 1 | 1 | 1 | 1 | $26,800 | 0 | 1 | $536 | 12 | $435 |
| 6 | 5 | 57 | 1 | 0 | 0 | 1 | $11,200 | 0 | 0 | $0 | 6 | $106 |
| 7 | 6 | 29 | 0 | 0 | 0 | 1 | $42,800 | 0 | 1 | $856 | 12 | $759 |
| 8 | 7 | 33 | 0 | 0 | 0 | 1 | $34,700 | 0 | 0 | $0 | 18 | $1,615 |
| 9 | 8 | 55 | 0 | 1 | 1 | 0 | $80,000 | 0 | 1 | $2,400 | 6 | $1,985 |
| 10 | 9 | 62 | 1 | 1 | 0 | 1 | $60,300 | 0 | 0 | $0 | 24 | $2,091 |
| 11 | 10 | 37 | 1 | 1 | 1 | 0 | $62,300 | 0 | 1 | $1,869 | 24 | $2,644 |

**Figure 8.15**

**Stepwise Options**

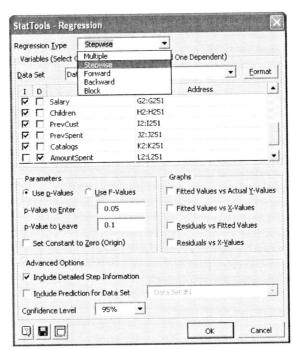

The stepwise output appears in Figure 8.16. It contains exactly the same information as multiple regression output, but it also has a bottom section that shows which variables entered in which order. In this case, the three variables Age, Married, and Own Home are not significant at the 0.05 level, so they did not enter the equation. If you try the forward stepwise method on this data set, using a p-value of 0.05 for entering, you will get exactly the same results. This is because no variables in the stepwise method ever exited after they entered. (In my experience, the stepwise method almost always yields the same results as the forward method.)

*Figure 8.16*

*Output from Stepwise and Forward Procedures*

| Summary | Multiple R | R-Square | Adjusted R-Square | StErr of Estimate | | |
|---|---|---|---|---|---|---|
| | 0.8885 | 0.7895 | 0.7834 | 422.517 | | |

| ANOVA Table | Degrees of Freedom | Sum of Squares | Mean of Squares | F-Ratio | p-Value | |
|---|---|---|---|---|---|---|
| Explained | 7 | 162035109 | 23147872.71 | 129.6650 | < 0.0001 | |
| Unexplained | 242 | 43201971.22 | 178520.5422 | | | |

| Regression Table | Coefficient | Standard Error | t-Value | p-Value | Confidence Interval 95% Lower | Upper |
|---|---|---|---|---|---|---|
| Constant | 269.864 | 108.560 | 2.4859 | 0.0136 | 56.022 | 483.707 |
| Salary | 0.015 | 0.001 | 11.1924 | < 0.0001 | 0.013 | 0.018 |
| Catalogs | 42.664 | 4.320 | 9.8751 | < 0.0001 | 34.154 | 51.174 |
| Children | -158.451 | 31.338 | -5.0562 | < 0.0001 | -220.181 | -96.721 |
| Close | -287.554 | 70.867 | -4.0576 | < 0.0001 | -427.149 | -147.959 |
| PrevCust | -724.065 | 91.587 | -7.9058 | < 0.0001 | -904.475 | -543.656 |
| PrevSpent | 0.470 | 0.078 | 6.0452 | < 0.0001 | 0.317 | 0.623 |
| Gender | -130.323 | 55.211 | -2.3604 | 0.0190 | -239.078 | -21.567 |

| Step Information | Multiple R | R-Square | Adjusted R-Square | StErr of Estimate | Enter or Exit |
|---|---|---|---|---|---|
| Salary | 0.6624 | 0.4387 | 0.4365 | 681.528 | Enter |
| Catalogs | 0.7718 | 0.5957 | 0.5924 | 579.609 | Enter |
| Children | 0.8256 | 0.6815 | 0.6777 | 515.446 | Enter |
| Close | 0.8540 | 0.7293 | 0.7249 | 476.200 | Enter |
| PrevCust | 0.8670 | 0.7516 | 0.7465 | 457.067 | Enter |
| PrevSpent | 0.8858 | 0.7847 | 0.7793 | 426.473 | Enter |
| Gender | 0.8885 | 0.7895 | 0.7834 | 422.517 | Enter |

For comparison, I also ran the backward stepwise method on this data set, using a p-value of 0.10 for leaving. The results appear in Figure 8.17. The first variable to leave is Age, then Married, and then Own Home. So the final equation is the same as with the stepwise and forward options. This is a coincidence. The results from these three methods are typically very similar, but there is no guarantee that they will always be the same.

**Figure 8.17**

**Output
from
Backward
Procedure**

| Summary | Multiple R | R-Square | Adjusted R-Square | StErr of Estimate | | |
|---|---|---|---|---|---|---|
| | 0.8885 | 0.7895 | 0.7834 | 422.517 | | |

| ANOVA Table | Degrees of Freedom | Sum of Squares | Mean of Squares | F-Ratio | p-Value | |
|---|---|---|---|---|---|---|
| Explained | 7 | 162035109 | 23147872.71 | 129.6650 | < 0.0001 | |
| Unexplained | 242 | 43201971.22 | 178520.5422 | | | |

| Regression Table | Coefficient | Standard Error | t-Value | p-Value | Confidence Interval 95% Lower | Upper |
|---|---|---|---|---|---|---|
| Constant | 269.864 | 108.560 | 2.4859 | 0.0136 | 56.022 | 483.707 |
| Gender | -130.323 | 55.211 | -2.3604 | 0.0190 | -239.078 | -21.567 |
| Close | -287.554 | 70.867 | -4.0576 | < 0.0001 | -427.149 | -147.959 |
| Salary | 0.015 | 0.001 | 11.1924 | < 0.0001 | 0.013 | 0.018 |
| Children | -158.451 | 31.338 | -5.0562 | < 0.0001 | -220.181 | -96.721 |
| PrevCust | -724.065 | 91.587 | -7.9058 | < 0.0001 | -904.475 | -543.656 |
| PrevSpent | 0.470 | 0.078 | 6.0452 | < 0.0001 | 0.317 | 0.623 |
| Catalogs | 42.664 | 4.320 | 9.8751 | < 0.0001 | 34.154 | 51.174 |

| Step Information | Multiple R | R-Square | Adjusted R-Square | StErr of Estimate | Exit Number |
|---|---|---|---|---|---|
| All Variables | 0.8893 | 0.7908 | 0.7820 | 423.858 | |
| Age | 0.8893 | 0.7908 | 0.7829 | 422.985 | 1 |
| Married | 0.8890 | 0.7903 | 0.7834 | 422.547 | 2 |
| Own Home | 0.8885 | 0.7895 | 0.7834 | 422.517 | 3 |

StatTools also implements one other stepwise procedure called the **block** method. This is not a completely standard regression procedure, but it is quite logical. There are many times when (1) you want variables to enter in a certain order, if they enter at all, and (2) variables come in blocks, so that it makes sense to enter *all* of the variables in the block or none of them.

To illustrate the StatTools block procedure, consider the expanded version of the salary data in Figure 8.18. (See the file **Salaries 4.xlsx**.) In addition to the interaction between Female and YrsExper, there are also interactions between Female and the EducLevel dummies. (I don't include the dummy or the interaction variable for education level 1; I designate this as the reference category for education level.) The interaction variables are sometimes called **second-order terms**, whereas the rest of the explanatory variables are **first-order** terms. It makes sense to have two blocks, one for the first-order terms and another for the second-order terms. The method first checks whether the first-order terms are significant as a whole. If not, it quits. If they are significant, they enter as a block and the second-order terms are checked for significance. They are then entered, as a block, only if the block as a whole is significant.

Figure 8.18

Salary Data

| | A | B | C | D | E | F | G | H | I | J | K | L |
|---|---|---|---|---|---|---|---|---|---|---|---|---|
| 1 | Employee | Age | Gender | EducLevel | YrsExper | Salary | Female | Female*YrsExper | EducLevel2 | EducLevel3 | Female*EducLevel2 | Female*EducLevel3 |
| 2 | 1 | 26 | Male | 3 | 3 | 32000 | 0 | 0 | 0 | 1 | 0 | 0 |
| 3 | 2 | 38 | Female | 1 | 14 | 39100 | 1 | 14 | 0 | 0 | 0 | 0 |
| 4 | 3 | 35 | Female | 1 | 12 | 33200 | 1 | 12 | 0 | 0 | 0 | 0 |
| 5 | 4 | 40 | Female | 2 | 8 | 30600 | 1 | 8 | 1 | 0 | 1 | 0 |
| 6 | 5 | 28 | Male | 3 | 3 | 29000 | 0 | 0 | 0 | 1 | 0 | 0 |
| 7 | 6 | 24 | Female | 3 | 3 | 30500 | 1 | 3 | 0 | 1 | 0 | 1 |
| 8 | 7 | 27 | Female | 3 | 4 | 30000 | 1 | 4 | 0 | 1 | 0 | 1 |
| 9 | 8 | 33 | Male | 3 | 8 | 27000 | 0 | 0 | 0 | 1 | 0 | 0 |
| 10 | 9 | 62 | Female | 1 | 4 | 34000 | 1 | 4 | 0 | 0 | 0 | 0 |
| 11 | 10 | 31 | Female | 3 | 9 | 29500 | 1 | 9 | 0 | 1 | 0 | 1 |

To implement the block procedure, select **Regression** from the **Regression & Classification** dropdown and fill in the resulting dialog box as in Figure 8.19, specifying two blocks and the corresponding variables in the blocks, and accepting the default p-value of 0.05 for block significance. The StatTools output in Figure 8.20 shows that both the first-order terms and the second-order (interaction) terms pass the significance test, so *all* variables enter. This does not imply that all variables in both blocks are significant—there are three relatively large p-values—but further fine-tuning of this equation is arguably not worth the effort.

Figure 8.19

Dialog Box
for Block
Procedure

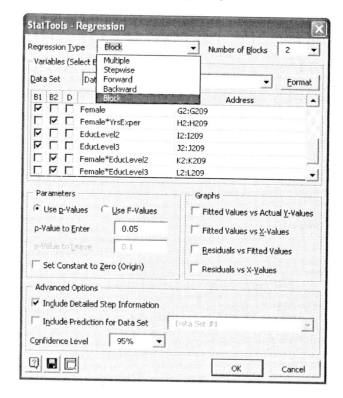

**Figure 8.20**

**Output from Block Procedure**

| Summary | Multiple R | R-Square | Adjusted R-Square | StErr of Estimate |
|---|---|---|---|---|
| | 0.8395 | 0.7047 | 0.6928 | 6238.616 |

| ANOVA Table | Degrees of Freedom | Sum of Squares | Mean of Squares | F-Ratio | p-Value |
|---|---|---|---|---|---|
| Explained | 8 | 18481960536 | 2310245067 | 59.3583 | < 0.0001 |
| Unexplained | 199 | 7745146694 | 38920335.15 | | |

| Regression Table | Coefficient | Standard Error | t-Value | p-Value | Confidence Interval 95% Lower | Upper |
|---|---|---|---|---|---|---|
| Constant | 14678.221 | 4537.905 | 3.234580876 | 0.0014 | 5729.669 | 23626.773 |
| Age | 84.293 | 61.210 | 1.377106742 | 0.1700 | -36.411 | 204.996 |
| YrsExper | 1436.576 | 104.915 | 13.69270194 | < 0.0001 | 1229.687 | 1643.465 |
| Female | 13091.736 | 4123.777 | 3.174695116 | 0.0017 | 4959.826 | 21223.646 |
| EducLevel2 | 5455.156 | 4497.326 | 1.212977705 | 0.2266 | -3413.375 | 14323.688 |
| EducLevel3 | 14810.881 | 3784.490 | 3.91357397 | 0.0001 | 7348.032 | 22273.731 |
| Female*YrsExper | -1126.896 | 128.544 | -8.766610184 | < 0.0001 | -1380.379 | -873.412 |
| Female*EducLevel2 | -5098.670 | 4775.175 | -1.067745049 | 0.2869 | -14515.107 | 4317.768 |
| Female*EducLevel3 | -9509.781 | 3972.091 | -2.394150101 | 0.0176 | -17342.571 | -1676.991 |

| Step Information | Multiple R | R-Square | Adjusted R-Square | StErr of Estimate | Entry Number |
|---|---|---|---|---|---|
| Block 1 | 0.7644 | 0.5842 | 0.5740 | 7347.130 | 1 |
| Block 2 | 0.8395 | 0.7047 | 0.6928 | 6238.616 | 2 |

**Notes**

- There must be some variation in the Y variable. If you try running a regression where the dependent variable is a constant, StatTools will warn you that this is not possible.

- There must be some variation in each of the selected X variables. If you try running a regression where at least one of the independent variables is a constant, StatTools will warn you of exact multicollinearity and will not let you continue.

- There must be at least two more observations than the number of X's in the equation. Otherwise, StatTools will issue an error message.

- In most data sets, the stepwise and forward procedures yield the same results. Usually, once a variable enters, it never leaves. However, take a look at the data set in the file **Surgical Units.xlsx**, with Log10_Y as the dependent variable and X1 through X4 as the independent variables. If you run the stepwise procedure with the default p-values, the variables enter in the order X4, X3, X2, and X1, but in the final step X4 leaves. This final step does not occur in the forward procedure—X4 remains in the equation. Nevertheless, the difference between the two final equations is minimal.

# 8.3 Logistic Regression

There are many situations where the Y variable to be explained is categorical. An important special case is when Y is **binary**, with possible values 0 and 1 that correspond to the two possible categories. Then regression really becomes a **classification problem**. The objective is to use the available X's to predict which category each observation is in, 1 or 0. For technical reasons, it is not a good idea to use regular least-squares regression when the dependent variable is binary. Instead, the appropriate method is a variation of regression called **logistic regression**. This method uses a nonlinear estimation technique to estimate the *probability* that a given observation is a 1, using the X's for this observation. To classify an observation, it uses a cutoff value of 0.5. If the estimated probability is greater than the cutoff value, the observation is classified as a 1; otherwise, it is classified as a 0.

Logistic regression actually estimates a linear equation for the **logit**, defined as the natural logarithm of $p/(1-p)$, where p is the probability of a 1. (This ratio, $p/(1-p)$, is called the **odds ratio**.) Therefore, the StatTools logistic regression output looks similar to multiple regression output. However, it must be interpreted differently.

To illustrate logistic regression, consider the data in Figure 8.21. (The full data set is in the file **Lasagna Triers.xlsx**.) A company is marketing a new frozen lasagna product, and it has demographic data on its customers. It wants to use the demographic data to predict who has tried the lasagna. Here, the HaveTried variable is the dependent variable, with value 1 for people who have tried the lasagna and 0 for those who haven't tried it.

*Figure 8.21*

*Lasagna Trier Data*

| | A | B | C | D | E | F | G |
|---|---|---|---|---|---|---|---|
| 1 | Person | Age | Weight | Income | Gender | LiveAlone | HaveTried |
| 2 | 1 | 27 | 167 | 40600 | 1 | 0 | 0 |
| 3 | 2 | 40 | 219 | 55200 | 1 | 0 | 0 |
| 4 | 3 | 31 | 190 | 48500 | 1 | 1 | 0 |
| 5 | 4 | 44 | 186 | 72100 | 0 | 0 | 0 |
| 6 | 5 | 45 | 152 | 60800 | 0 | 0 | 0 |
| 7 | 6 | 52 | 182 | 67600 | 1 | 0 | 0 |
| 8 | 7 | 38 | 184 | 45300 | 0 | 0 | 0 |
| 9 | 8 | 35 | 227 | 54200 | 0 | 0 | 0 |
| 10 | 9 | 37 | 191 | 65100 | 0 | 0 | 0 |
| 11 | 10 | 41 | 145 | 49300 | 1 | 0 | 0 |

To implement logistic regression, select **Logistic Regression** from the **Regression & Classification** dropdown. This brings up the dialog box in Figure 8.22, where you should accept the default analysis type in the top dropdown box, select the variables (just like in multiple regression), and check any options you want at the bottom. I suggest these particular options. However, you can also select the Prediction option, as I will discuss shortly.

---

**Figure 8.22**

**Dialog Box for Logistic Regression**

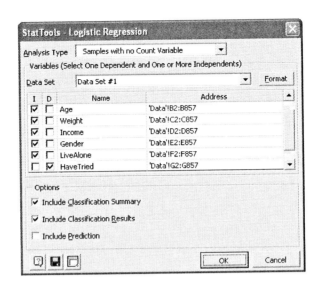

The logistic regression output from StatTools comes in two parts. The basic regression output appears in Figure 8.23. Its second section essentially spells out the estimated equation for the logit and is very similar to multiple regression output. The top section is similar to the summary section for multiple regression. Because these outputs are not as familiar to most users as the usual regression statistics, StatTools adds plenty of cell comments to explain their meaning. (One of these cell comments is shown in the figure. You can refer to the file for the others.) The bottom part of this output contains classification results. They indicate that the model correctly classifies 401 of the 495 1's and 239 of the 361 0's. This results in a correct classification rate of 74.8%. The last two percentages indicate how good this is. Because 57.8% of the observations are 1's, you could achieve a correct classification rate of 57.8% simply by classifying *all* observations as 1's. The 74.8% rate in the output is 40.2% of the way from the base 57.8% rate to a perfect 100% rate.

**Figure 8.23**

**Logistic Regression Output**

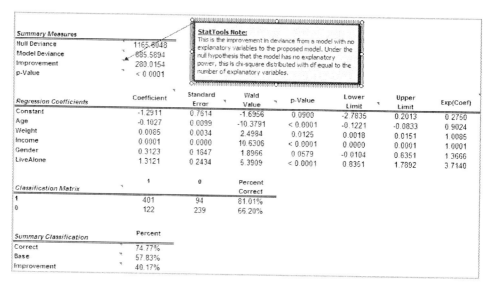

| Summary Measures | |
|---|---|
| Null Deviance | 1165.6048 |
| Model Deviance | 885.5894 |
| Improvement | 280.0154 |
| p-Value | < 0.0001 |

**StatTools Note:**
This is the improvement in deviance from a model with no explanatory variables to the proposed model. Under the null hypothesis that the model has no explanatory power, this is chi-square distributed with df equal to the number of explanatory variables.

| Regression Coefficients | Coefficient | Standard Error | Wald Value | p-Value | Lower Limit | Upper Limit | Exp(Coef) |
|---|---|---|---|---|---|---|---|
| Constant | -1.2911 | 0.7614 | -1.6956 | 0.0900 | -2.7835 | 0.2013 | 0.2750 |
| Age | -0.1027 | 0.0099 | -10.3791 | < 0.0001 | -0.1221 | -0.0833 | 0.9024 |
| Weight | 0.0085 | 0.0034 | 2.4984 | 0.0125 | 0.0018 | 0.0151 | 1.0085 |
| Income | 0.0001 | 0.0000 | 10.6306 | < 0.0001 | 0.0000 | 0.0001 | 1.0001 |
| Gender | 0.3123 | 0.1647 | 1.8966 | 0.0579 | -0.0104 | 0.6351 | 1.3666 |
| LiveAlone | 1.3121 | 0.2434 | 5.3909 | < 0.0001 | 0.8351 | 1.7892 | 3.7140 |

| Classification Matrix | 1 | 0 | Percent Correct |
|---|---|---|---|
| 1 | 401 | 94 | 81.01% |
| 0 | 122 | 239 | 66.20% |

| Summary Classification | Percent |
|---|---|
| Correct | 74.77% |
| Base | 57.83% |
| Improvement | 40.17% |

The second part of the output, shown in Figure 8.24, lists estimated probabilities and classifications. For example, the estimated probability that observation 3 is a 1 is 0.817. Because this is greater than the cutoff of 0.5, this observation is classified as a 1. In this case, it is wrong—observation 3 is actually a 0.

**Figure 8.24**

**Probabilities and Classifications**

| Probabilities and Classifications | Age | Weight | Income | Gender | LiveAlone | Probability | Analysis Class | Original Class |
|---|---|---|---|---|---|---|---|---|
| 1 | 27 | 167 | 40600 | 1 | 0 | 48.81% | 0 | 0 |
| 2 | 40 | 219 | 55200 | 1 | 0 | 47.03% | 0 | 0 |
| 3 | 31 | 190 | 48500 | 1 | 1 | 81.66% | 1 | 0 |
| 4 | 44 | 186 | 72100 | 0 | 0 | 45.75% | 0 | 0 |
| 5 | 46 | 152 | 60800 | 0 | 0 | 23.19% | 0 | 0 |
| 6 | 52 | 182 | 67600 | 1 | 0 | 27.56% | 0 | 0 |

This Prediction option for logistic regression works just like the in multiple regression, the only difference being that you do not get 95% prediction intervals; you get only classifications—1 or 0—for the observations in the prediction data set. To illustrate, I created the second data set in Figure 8.25, with the HaveTried values missing, and filled in the logistic regression dialog box as in Figure 8.26. The prediction results appear in Figure 8.27. StatTools estimates the probability that each observation is a 1. If this estimate is greater than the cutoff value of 0.5, it records a 1 in the HaveTried column. Otherwise, it records a 0.

**Figure 8.25**

**Data for Prediction**

| | I | J | K | L | M | N | O |
|---|---|---|---|---|---|---|---|
| 1 | Person | Age | Weight | Income | Gender | LiveAlone | HaveTried |
| 2 | 1 | 38 | 184 | 85400 | 1 | 0 | |
| 3 | 2 | 52 | 171 | 56200 | 1 | 1 | |
| 4 | 3 | 47 | 205 | 44200 | 0 | 0 | |

**Figure 8.26**

**Dialog Box with Prediction Option**

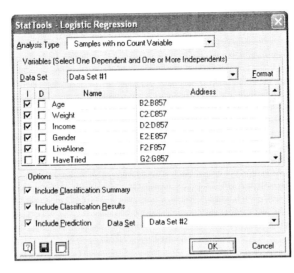

**Figure 8.27**

**Prediction Results**

| | I | J | K | L | M | N | O |
|---|---|---|---|---|---|---|---|
| 1 | Person | Age | Weight | Income | Gender | LiveAlone | HaveTried |
| 2 | 1 | 38 | 184 | 85400 | 1 | 0 | 1 |
| 3 | 2 | 52 | 171 | 56200 | 1 | 1 | 0 |
| 4 | 3 | 47 | 205 | 44200 | 0 | 0 | 0 |

The lasagna data has observations for individual people, one row per person. Sometimes the data set shows a group of observations in each row. For example, consider the data set in Figure 8.28. (See the file **Credit Results.xlsx**.) A large number or people (1800) are classified as one of two age categories and as one of three income categories. For each of the six age–income joint categories, the number of people in the category and the number of these with bad credit ratings are listed. The goal is to use logistic regression to predict whether a person's credit rating is bad based on the person's age and income categories. Note that this is really just a condensed form of the type of data set in the lasagna example. It could be replaced with a large data set with 1800 rows. For example, 500 of these rows would correspond to young, low-income people; 25 of these 500 rows would have 1 for the dependent variable and 475 would have 0. The distinguishing features is that the condensed data set has a **count variable** (the Number variable). This count variable specifies the number of rows in the expanded data set that would have equivalent values of the X's.

*Figure 8.28*

*Data with
Count
Variable*

| | A | B | C | D | E | F | G | H |
|---|---|---|---|---|---|---|---|---|
| 1 | Joint category | Age | Income | Number | NumberBad | Young | LowInc | MidInc |
| 2 | 1 | Young | Low | 500 | 25 | 1 | 1 | 0 |
| 3 | 2 | Young | Middle | 300 | 9 | 1 | 0 | 1 |
| 4 | 3 | Young | High | 200 | 2 | 1 | 0 | 0 |
| 5 | 4 | Old | Low | 200 | 8 | 0 | 1 | 0 |
| 6 | 5 | Old | Middle | 400 | 4 | 0 | 0 | 1 |
| 7 | 6 | Old | High | 200 | 1 | 0 | 0 | 0 |

If the data set has a count variable, you should fill in the logistic regression dialog box as in Figure 8.29, specifying Number as the count variable and NumberBad as the dependent variable. Note that the Young, LowInc, and MidInc variables are actually dummies based on the character variables Age and Income. These dummies are used as the independent variables in the logistic regression.

*Figure 8.29*

*Dialog Box
with Count
Variable
Option*

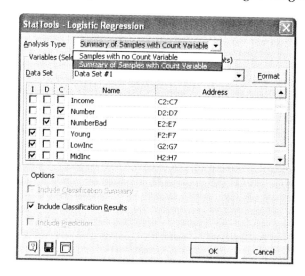

The logistic regression output appears in Figure 8.30. For each joint category, it lists the estimated probability of a bad credit rating. For example, the estimated probability for a young, low-income person is 0.0535. You can interpret this as the probability that a typical young, low-income person has a bad credit rating. Equivalently, you can interpret it as the fraction of all young, low-income people who have a bad credit rating.

**Figure 8.30**

**Logistic Regression Output**

| Summary Measures | |
|---|---|
| Null Deviance | 23.487 |
| Model Deviance | 1.502 |
| Improvement | 21.985 |
| p-Value | < 0.0001 |

| Regression Coefficients | Coefficient | Standard Error | Wald Value | p-Value | Lower Limit | Upper Limit | Exp(Coef) |
|---|---|---|---|---|---|---|---|
| Constant | -5.204 | 0.618 | -8.416 | < 0.0001 | -6.415 | -3.992 | 0.005 |
| Young | 0.560 | 0.339 | 1.654 | 0.0982 | -0.104 | 1.224 | 1.751 |
| LowInc | 1.770 | 0.609 | 2.905 | 0.0037 | 0.576 | 2.965 | 5.872 |
| MidInc | 0.959 | 0.644 | 1.488 | 0.1368 | -0.304 | 2.221 | 2.608 |

| Probabilities and Classifications | Young | LowInc | MidInc | Summary Count | Total Count | Probability |
|---|---|---|---|---|---|---|
| 1 | 1 | 1 | 0 | 25 | 500 | 5.35% |
| 2 | 1 | 0 | 1 | 9 | 300 | 2.45% |
| 3 | 1 | 0 | 0 | 2 | 200 | 0.95% |
| 4 | 0 | 1 | 0 | 8 | 200 | 3.13% |
| 5 | 0 | 0 | 1 | 4 | 400 | 1.41% |
| 6 | 0 | 0 | 0 | 1 | 200 | 0.55% |

# 8.4 Discriminant Analysis

Discriminant analysis is an alternative to logistic regression for classifying observations into two or more categories. As with logistic regression, it uses values on explanatory variables (the X's) to make classifications, but the technique itself is quite different. In the two-group case, where there are only two categories, it estimates a line based on the X's that **maximally separates** the two groups. It then classifies any observation into one of the two groups, depending on which side of the line the observation is on.

Unlike logistic regression, the StatTools implementation of discriminant analysis allows you to have more than two categories. In this case, its classifications are based on **statistical distance**, a technical modification of the usual Euclidean distance measure that accounts for variances and covariances of the X's. For any observation, it calculates the statistical distance from the observation to the group mean for each group. Then it classifies this observation into the group with the smallest statistical distance. Essentially, an observation is classified as the group to which it corresponds most closely in terms of its X values.

In the two-group case, there are two parameters of discriminant analysis that StatTools allows you to modify. The first is the prior probability of being a 0. (I will continue to refer to one group as the 1's and the other group as the 0's.) By default this prior probability is 0.5—you believe that half of the observations in the population are 1's and the other half are 0's. If this is clearly not the case, you can enter your own prior probability of a 0. Second, you can enter misclassification costs. By default, there is no misclassification cost for classifying an observation correctly, and the cost of misclassifying a 1 as a 0 is the same as the cost of misclassifying a 0 as a 1. You can change these costs if you like.

I illustrate a two-group discriminant analysis with the same lasagna data from the previous section. To run the analysis, select **Discriminant Analysis** from the **Regression & Classification** dropdown and fill in the resulting dialog box as in Figure 8.31. Note that the method relies heavily on variance–covariance matrices calculated for the two groups. You can view these by checking the second option in the bottom section. You can also select the Include Prediction to perform exactly the same type of prediction on new data that was illustrated for logistic regression.

Figure 8.31

Dialog Box
for
Discriminant
Analysis

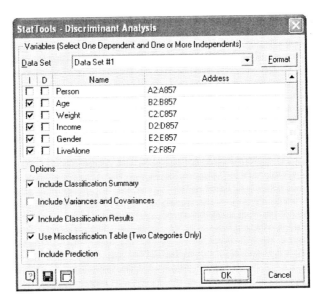

Once you click on OK, you get to modify the default prior probability and misclassification costs, as shown in Figure 8.32. For the sake of illustration, I changed the prior probability of being a lasagna non-trier to 0.4, and I made the cost of misclassifying a non-trier as a trier twice as large as the opposite misclassification cost. Of course, these always depend on an assessment of the *actual* costs involved.

Figure 8.32

Dialog Box
for
Additional
Parameters

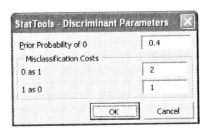

The StatTools output appears in Figures 8.33 and 8.34. The sample summary in Figure 8.33 lets you compare the means of the X's for the two groups. Then it shows the coefficients of the line, called the **discriminant function**, used for classification, as well as the classification results. (These results are somewhat different from the logistic regression classification results in Figure 8.23 for the same data. This is due mainly to the different prior probability and misclassification costs used here.) The output in Figure 8.34 shows the value of the discriminant function (under Discrim) for each observation. If this Discrim value is less than some cutoff value (not shown in the output), the observation is classified as a 1; otherwise, it is classified as a 0. The output also shows the statistical distance from each observation to each group mean. (However, it turns out that these statistical distances cannot be used directly for classification in the two-group case unless the prior probability is 0.5 and the two misclassification costs are equal.)

**Figure 8.33**

**Discriminant Analysis Output**

| Setup Variables | Prior Probability | Misclassification Cost 0 | 1 |
|---|---|---|---|
| 0 | 0.4 | 0 | 2 |
| 1 | 0.6 | 1 | 0 |

| Sample Summary | Sample Size | Mean Age | Mean Weight | Mean Income | Mean Gender | Mean LiveAlone |
|---|---|---|---|---|---|---|
| 0 | 361 | 42.524 | 190.717 | 58404.709 | 0.496 | 0.102 |
| 1 | 495 | 36.055 | 194.079 | 71892.929 | 0.564 | 0.218 |

| Discriminant Function | Coefficient |
|---|---|
| Age | 0.1003 |
| Weight | -0.0074 |
| Income | -0.0001 |
| Gender | -0.3219 |
| LiveAlone | -1.1652 |

| Classification Matrix | 0 | 1 | Correct |
|---|---|---|---|
| 0 | 292 | 69 | 80.9% |
| 1 | 184 | 311 | 62.8% |

| Summary Classification | |
|---|---|
| Correct | 70.4% |
| Base | 57.8% |
| Improvement | 29.9% |

**Figure 8.34**

**Statistical Distances and Classifications**

| Statistical Distance | Age | Weight | Income | Gender | LiveAlone | StatDist 0 | StatDist 1 | Discrim | Original Class | Analysis Class |
|---|---|---|---|---|---|---|---|---|---|---|
| 1 | 27 | 167 | 40600 | 1 | 0 | 2.289 | 2.411 | -0.993 | 0 | 0 |
| 2 | 40 | 219 | 55200 | 1 | 0 | 1.609 | 1.859 | -0.845 | 0 | 0 |
| 3 | 31 | 190 | 48500 | 1 | 1 | 3.030 | 2.656 | -2.344 | 0 | 1 |
| 4 | 44 | 186 | 72100 | 0 | 0 | 1.298 | 1.645 | -0.769 | 0 | 0 |
| 5 | 45 | 152 | 60800 | 0 | 0 | 1.937 | 2.582 | 0.180 | 0 | 0 |
| 6 | 52 | 182 | 67600 | 1 | 0 | 1.591 | 2.247 | -0.021 | 0 | 0 |

As mentioned earlier, StatTools can handle more than two groups with its discriminant analysis procedure. For example, consider the data in Figure 8.35. (See the full data set in the file **Textbook Adoptions.xlsx**.) This data set lists information on several universities. For each university, it also lists the status of a particular textbook—whether the book has never been adopted, is still being used, or was adopted but is no longer used. The publisher of the textbook would like to classify these universities in an attempt to understand why some never adopt the book and why some discontinue using it.

**Figure 8.35**

**Textbook Adoption Data**

| | A | B | C | D | E | F | G | H |
|---|---|---|---|---|---|---|---|---|
| 1 | University | Enrollment | AvgSAT | PctTenure | PCLabs | PctOwnPC | Tuition | Status |
| 2 | 1 | 12429 | 1222 | 90.7% | 186 | 54.5% | 17700 | Never |
| 3 | 2 | 20707 | 974 | 68.4% | 93 | 44.4% | 11000 | Still |
| 4 | 3 | 18338 | 841 | 50.7% | 127 | 24.8% | 7600 | NoMore |
| 5 | 4 | 15750 | 854 | 57.5% | 153 | 59.3% | 15400 | Still |
| 6 | 5 | 15416 | 1098 | 77.1% | 179 | 49.4% | 15700 | Never |
| 7 | 6 | 14612 | 824 | 49.8% | 112 | 46.1% | 8000 | NoMore |
| 8 | 7 | 14520 | 912 | 60.1% | 127 | 35.0% | 9400 | NoMore |
| 9 | 8 | 16346 | 988 | 60.2% | 133 | 58.6% | 12300 | Still |
| 10 | 9 | 15580 | 939 | 61.2% | 78 | 43.6% | 8800 | NoMore |
| 11 | 10 | 19029 | 1067 | 72.0% | 148 | 61.1% | 14400 | Still |

To run the analysis, you fill in the discriminant analysis dialog box exactly as in the two-group case. However, there are now no options for prior probabilities or misclassification costs. The prior probabilities are all assumed to be equal, as are the various misclassification costs.

The resulting output appears in Figures 8.36 and 8.37. There is only one basic difference from the two-group case. There is now no discriminant function listed. Instead, the classification is based on statistical distance. For example, the statistical distances from university 1 to the means of the Never, NoMore, and Still groups are 2.722, 6.198, and 6.410. Because the smallest of these is 2.722, university 1 is classified as Never—which happens to be correct. In addition, a comparison of the sample means for the groups, listed at the top of Figure 8.36, provides some indication of how the groups differ. For example, the Never group has by far the largest SAT scores, the percentage of tenured faculty, and the largest tuitions. These variables tend to separate the Never group from the other two groups. Similarly, the Still and NoMore groups tend be separated from one another on the number of PC labs and the percentage of students who own PCs.

**Figure 8.36**

**Discriminant Analysis Output**

| Sample Summary | Sample Size | Mean Enrollment | Mean AvgSAT | Mean PctTenure | Mean PCLabs | Mean PctOwnPC | Mean Tuition |
|---|---|---|---|---|---|---|---|
| Never | 40 | 14799.050 | 1134.275 | 0.806 | 148.150 | 0.549 | 14997.500 |
| NoMore | 37 | 14888.459 | 921.730 | 0.599 | 101.622 | 0.440 | 9878.378 |
| Still | 42 | 19575.595 | 950.143 | 0.595 | 153.286 | 0.520 | 9680.952 |

| Classification Matrix | Never | NoMore | Still | Correct |
|---|---|---|---|---|
| Never | 39 | 0 | 1 | 0.975 |
| NoMore | 0 | 34 | 3 | 0.442 |
| Still | 0 | 3 | 39 | 0.328 |

| Summary Classification | |
|---|---|
| Correct | 94.1% |
| Base | 35.3% |
| Improvement | 90.9% |

**Figure 8.37**

**Statistical Distances and Classifications**

| Statistical Distance | Enrollment | AvgSAT | PctTenure | PCLabs | PctOwnPC | Tuition | StatDist Never | StatDist NoMore | StatDist Still | Original Class | Analysis Class |
|---|---|---|---|---|---|---|---|---|---|---|---|
| 1 | 12429 | 1222 | 0.907 | 186 | 0.545 | 17700 | 2.722 | 6.198 | 6.410 | Never | Never |
| 2 | 20707 | 974 | 0.684 | 93 | 0.444 | 11000 | 4.339 | 4.000 | 3.805 | Still | Still |
| 3 | 18338 | 841 | 0.507 | 127 | 0.248 | 7600 | 5.133 | 2.549 | 3.443 | NoMore | NoMore |
| 4 | 15750 | 854 | 0.575 | 153 | 0.593 | 15400 | 5.418 | 3.599 | 3.401 | Still | Still |
| 5 | 15416 | 1098 | 0.771 | 179 | 0.494 | 15700 | 1.486 | 4.132 | 4.011 | Never | Never |
| 6 | 14612 | 824 | 0.498 | 112 | 0.461 | 8000 | 5.739 | 2.353 | 3.593 | NoMore | NoMore |

## Notes

- Logistic regression and discriminant analysis are only two of several classification methods. Others include classification trees, neural networks, and naïve Bayes. All of these methods have their relative advantages, and analysts tend to have their favorites. For now, logistic regression and discriminant analysis are the only two implemented by StatTools.

# Chapter 9: Time Series and Forecasting

*Patterns*

**Time Series and Forecasting Icon**

## 9.1 Introduction

Working with time series data presents a unique challenge. The goals are typically to understand the patterns in historical data and to forecast these patterns into the future. From a practical standpoint, there are two complications: randomness (or noise) in the historical data, and the uncertainty of whether history will repeat itself in the future. The noise in the historical data often makes it difficult to detect the underlying patterns. The uncertainty of whether history will repeat itself means that even if the historical patterns can be detected, there is no guarantee that future forecasts based on these will be accurate—and they often aren't. Nevertheless, time series analysis and forecasting are extremely important in the business world and in other areas, so the tools discussed in this chapter find many uses.

## 9.2 Time Series Graphs

The best place to start with any time series analysis is with a **time series graph**. This shows the movement of one or more time series variables through time. This type of graph allows you to spot any obvious trends or seasonal patterns.

The data in Figure 9.1 represent monthly sales of stereos (in $1000s) for a chain of electronics stores. (The data actually extend through December 2008. The full data set is in the file **Stereo Sales.xlsx**.) This is a common setup for time series data: one column for dates and another for the time series variable. To graph these data through time, select **Time Series Graphs** from the **Time Series & Forecasting** dropdown and fill in the resulting dialog box as in Figure 9.2. The top dropdown list in this dialog box allows you to choose a graph with or without date labels. If there is a date variable in the data set, it is a good idea to use it for labeling.

*Figure 9.1*

*Stereo*
*Sales*

| | A | B |
|---|---|---|
| 1 | Month | Sales |
| 2 | Jan-05 | 226 |
| 3 | Feb-05 | 254 |
| 4 | Mar-05 | 204 |
| 5 | Apr-05 | 193 |
| 6 | May-05 | 191 |
| 7 | Jun-05 | 166 |
| 8 | Jul-05 | 175 |
| 9 | Aug-05 | 217 |
| 10 | Sep-05 | 167 |
| 11 | Oct-05 | 192 |
| 12 | Nov-05 | 127 |
| 13 | Dec-05 | 148 |

*Figure 9.2*

*Dialog Box*
*for Graph*
*with Date*
*Labels*

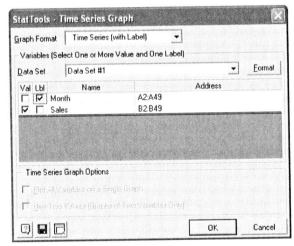

The resulting time series graph is shown in Figure 9.3. It appears that stereo sales are really going nowhere—there are no clear trends or seasonal patterns.

Figure 9.3

Time Series
Graph of
Stereo
Sales

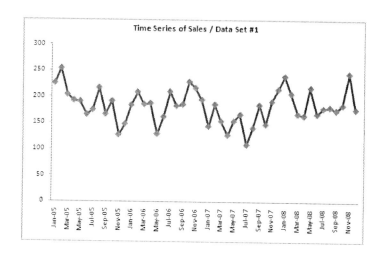

The data in Figure 9.4 (an excerpt from the file **Two Product Sales.xlsx**) represent sales (in $1000s) for two of a company's products. This data set allows me to illustrate two other features of the StatTools Time Series Graph procedure. First, there is no date variable. Therefore, when you fill in the dialog box in Figure 9.5, you must select the **without Label** option. Second, the company might want to plot time series of both products on the *same* graph. StatTools allows any number of time series variables to be plotted on the same graph. However, it offers a special option when there are exactly two variables of very different magnitudes, as there are here. If sales of these two products are plotted on the same scale, then the small sales of product 2 will be swamped by the larger sales of product 2. However, by checking the bottom option in the dialog box, you can obtain different scales for the two variables. (Again, this option is available only when you select exactly *two* variables to plot.)

Figure 9.4

Sales of
Two
Products

| | A | B | C |
|---|---|---|---|
| 1 | Month | Product1 | Product2 |
| 2 | Jan-06 | 125.2 | 5.3 |
| 3 | Feb-06 | 124.3 | 5.5 |
| 4 | Mar-06 | 118 | 5.5 |
| 5 | Apr-06 | 115.2 | 6.8 |
| 6 | May-06 | 127.2 | 6.5 |
| 7 | Jun-06 | 129 | 6.9 |
| 8 | Jul-06 | 135.9 | 6.8 |
| 9 | Aug-06 | 131.5 | 6.7 |
| 10 | Sep-06 | 130 | 6.6 |

Figure 9.5

Dialog Box
for Graph
for Two
Variables
with
Different
Scales

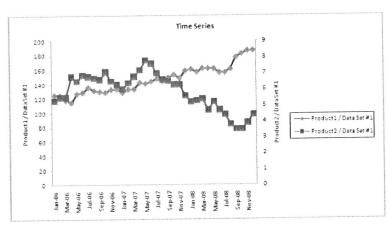

The resulting time series graph appears in Figure 9.6. It uses the left-hand scale for product 1 and the right-hand scale for product 2. Note that product 1 sales have basically been trending downward recently, exactly the opposite of product 2 sales.

Figure 9.6

Time Series
of Sales of
Both
Products

### Notes

- As is apparent from Figure 9.6, StatTools labels the horizontal axis with the consecutive integers 1, 2, 3, etc. if the **without Label** option is selected. It is clearly better to use date labels if a date variable is available.

- If you select two or more variables to plot, you can choose to plot them on the same graph or on separate graphs. If you choose to plot three or more variables on the same graph, they automatically share the same scale.

# 9.3 Autocorrelation

The values of a time series variable are often **autocorrelated**. This means that they are literally correlated with themselves. For example, if a monthly variable has a large autocorrelation at lag 1, then observations in successive months are correlated—if March sales are high (or low), April sales will tend to be high (or low). Or if this variable has a large autocorrelation at lag 12, then observations separated by 12 months are correlated—if March sales are high (or low) in 2008, then March sales in 2009 will tend to be high (or low). It is actually possible to calculate an autocorrelation for *any* lag to see whether observations separated by that many periods are correlated, but small lags such as 1, 2, and 3, or seasonal lags such as 12 or 24, are usually of most interest.

Autocorrelation presents complications for time series analysis, and advanced techniques are required to deal with these complications. Therefore, it is useful to check whether significant autocorrelations are present. StatTools allows you to do this. For example, to check for autocorrelations in the stereo sales data from the previous section, select **Autocorrelation** from the **Time Series & Forecasting** dropdown and fill in the resulting dialog box as in Figure 9.7. There are two options worth noting. First, StatTools automatically sets the number of lags at approximately one-quarter of the number of observations. For example, with 48 observations, StatTools selects 12 lags by default. You can override this number, but it is not advisable to request *more* than this many lags. Second, StatTools produces an autocorrelation chart, called a **correlogram**, by default. It is a good idea to check this option.

*Figure 9.7*

*Dialog Box for Autocorrelations*

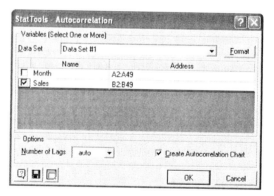

The output includes the list of autocorrelations in Figure 9.8 and the correlogram in Figure 9.9. Because of random variation, autocorrelations are almost never exactly equal to 0, so it is useful to test whether they are large enough to be statistically significant. StatTools makes this check and boldfaces significant autocorrelations. Note that the autocorrelation at lag 1 is the only significant autocorrelation for this data set. Because it is positive, sales in successive months tend to be correlated. Nevertheless, an autocorrelation of 0.349 is not all that large, so a high sales value in May, say, could very easily be followed by a low sales value in June.

**Figure 9.8**

**Table of Autocorrelations**

| Autocorrelation Table | Sales Data Set #1 |
|---|---|
| Number of Values | 48 |
| Standard Error | 0.1443 |
| Lag #1 | 0.3492 |
| Lag #2 | 0.0772 |
| Lag #3 | 0.0814 |
| Lag #4 | -0.0095 |
| Lag #5 | -0.1353 |
| Lag #6 | 0.0206 |
| Lag #7 | -0.1494 |
| Lag #8 | -0.1492 |
| Lag #9 | -0.2626 |
| Lag #10 | -0.1792 |
| Lag #11 | 0.0121 |
| Lag #12 | -0.0516 |

**Figure 9.9**

**Correlogram**

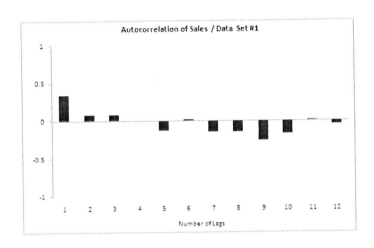

**Notes**

- To calculate autocorrelations, StatTools uses a slightly modified version of the usual correlation formula to correlate the original time series with lagged versions of itself. In spite of this modification, autocorrelations are still in the range from –1 to +1.

- Significant *positive* autocorrelations are much more common in real data than significant *negative* autocorrelations, but both are possible.

# 9.4 Runs Test for Randomness

The objective in using a forecasting technique on some time series variable is to "squeeze out" all predictable patterns from the data, so that the only thing left is unpredictable random noise. The question then is how to know whether a given time series is random, with no predictable patterns. One useful way to test a series for randomness is the **runs test**.

To understand the runs test, consider a simple experiment of coin flipping. Suppose you flip a coin 20 times and observe 10 heads in a row followed by 10 tails in a row. You got 10 heads and 10 tails, as expected, but you would be pretty suspicious about these results. The problem is that you observed only two runs, where a **run** is defined as a sequence of the same outcome. You would expect heads and tails to alternate more frequently, so you would expect more than two runs. On the other hand, if the outcomes alternated head, tail, head, tail, etc. for all 20 flips, there would be 20 runs, a suspiciously large number. So for a **random** sequence of flips, you would expect some intermediate number of runs.

It is possible to test for randomness of time series data in basically the same way. You choose a "middle" value, such as the mean or the median of the series, and then define a run as a sequence of values that stays above (or below) this middle value. You then count the number of runs and compare this to what you would expect if the series were really random. Statisticians have determined the distribution of the number of runs under an assumption of randomness, and they have used this as the basis for the runs test.

To illustrate the runs test, consider again use the stereo sales data from Section 9.2 (in the file **Stereo Sales.xlsx**). Because the time series graph of sales in Figure 9.3 does not appear to have much of a pattern, it is conceivable that this series is really unpredictable randomness. To perform the test, select **Runs Test for Randomness** from the **Time Series & Forecasting** dropdown and fill in the resulting dialog box as in Figure 9.10. Note that you can base the test on runs about the mean of the series, the median, or even your own custom cutoff value. It is a good idea to use either the mean or the median.

Figure 9.10

Dialog Box
for Runs
Test

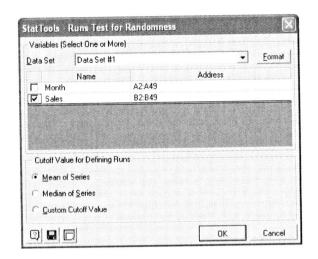

The output from the test appears in Figure 9.11. For these 48 observations, there are 20 runs about the mean. Evidently, this is slightly fewer than the expected number, 24.833, for a random series. However, the difference is not all that large according to the relatively high p-value of 0.155. Unless this p-value is less than the traditional significance levels (0.10 or 0.05, say), the null hypothesis of randomness cannot be rejected. In other words, there is not enough evidence in this time series to conclude a *lack* of randomness.

Figure 9.11

Output
from Runs
Test

| Runs Test for Randomness | Sales Data Set #1 |
| --- | --- |
| Observations | 48 |
| Below Mean | 22 |
| Above Mean | 26 |
| Number of Runs | 20 |
| Mean | 182.67 |
| E(R) | 24.833 |
| StdDev(R) | 3.403 |
| Z-Value | -1.420 |
| P-Value (two-tailed) | 0.155 |

# 9.5 Forecasting

There are many forecasting techniques that have been devised by statisticians, ranging from simple to complex, and there is no single technique that always produces the best forecasts. StatTools implements two of the most popular techniques: **moving averages** and **exponential smoothing**. Both of these are **smoothing methods**, in that they attempt to smooth out the random ups and downs—the noise—inherent in most time series, so that the future forecasts are based on the underlying patterns in the historical series. Actually, there are many exponential smoothing methods available, and StatTools implements three of these: **simple exponential smoothing**, **Holt's method** (for trend), and **Winters' method** (for seasonality). In addition, it implements a method for **deseasonalizing** a time series with seasonality, so that the deseasonalized series can then be forecasted with any of the available methods.

Each of these forecasting methods builds a model to forecast the historical period. In that way, you can see how well the model tracks the historical data. Presumably, a method that tracks the historical data well has a better chance of providing accurate forecasts of the future. However, you typically do not want to track every up and down of the historical series, because there is no sense in tracking random noise. This is why smoothing methods are popular. To gauge how well the forecasting model is working, StatTools lets you **hold out** the last part of the series. For example, if the data set consists of quarterly data for 1992–2008, you might hold out the last 8 quarters. Then you can build the model based on the data for 1992–2006 and use it to forecast the known data for 2007–2008. It is always interesting to see whether the model works as well for the holdout period as for the period on which it is based. In addition, StatTools also lets you forecast for *future* periods—for example, the period 2009–2010. Unlike the holdout period, observations for future periods are unknown at the time the forecast model is built.

To see how well the model's forecasts track the historical series, StatTools calculates three common measures of forecast errors:

- **MAE** (mean absolute error): average of the absolute errors

- **RMSE** (root mean square error): square root of the average of the squared errors

- **MAPE** (mean absolute percentage error): average of the absolute percentage errors

Although StatTools reports all three of these measures, a forecasting model that makes one of them small typically makes *all* of them small. Therefore, you can focus on any one of these measures.

## Moving Averages

The **moving averages** method is very simple to explain. Consider monthly data. Then the moving averages forecast for any month is the average of the observations in the preceding few months. The number of observations in each average is called the **span**, a parameter you can choose. Because of the averaging effect, a larger span results in more smoothing. As an example, if you choose a span of 3, then the forecast for May is the average of the observations from February, March, and April, the forecast for June is the average of the observations from March, April, and May, and so on. This explains the term *moving* averages.

To illustrate the moving averages method, consider the data in Figure 9.12 on weekly hardware dollar sales at a discount store such as Target or Kmart. (There are actually 104 weeks of data. See the file **Hardware Sales.xlsx** for the full data set.) The time series graph in Figure 9.13 indicates that sales are "meandering" through time—there is no obvious trend or seasonal pattern. This is the type of series that the moving averages method is well suited to. If there is a clear trend, the moving averages typically lag behind it, and if there is a seasonal pattern, the moving averages typically miss it altogether.

*Figure 9.12*

*Weekly Hardware Sales*

| | A | B |
|---|---|---|
| 1 | Week | Sales |
| 2 | 1 | 1526 |
| 3 | 2 | 1929 |
| 4 | 3 | 1704 |
| 5 | 4 | 1423 |
| 6 | 5 | 1430 |
| 7 | 6 | 1410 |
| 8 | 7 | 1478 |
| 9 | 8 | 1698 |
| 10 | 9 | 2223 |
| 11 | 10 | 2420 |

*Figure 9.13*

*Time Series Graph of Hardware Sales*

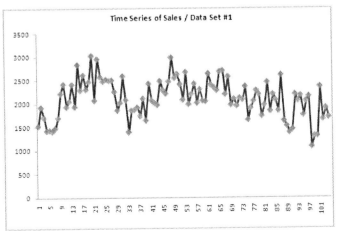

To forecast this series with moving averages, select **Forecast** from the **Time Series & Forecasting** dropdown. This brings up the dialog box in Figure 9.14. There are three tabs in the bottom section of this dialog box. The first tab, shown in Figure 9.14, is where you specify the number of future forecasts (if any), the number of periods to hold out (if any), and the forecasting method to use. Here, I have specified 5 future weeks, 10 weeks for holdout, and the moving averages method with a span of 6 weeks. This last parameter, the span, is particularly important because it determines the amount of smoothing. Some trial and error with the span is typically required to obtain the best forecasts. (I do not claim that a span of 6 is best for this series.)

*Figure 9.14*

*Forecast Settings Tab in Forecasting Dialog Box*

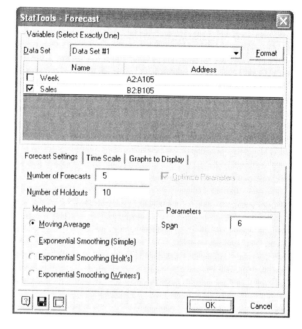

The other two tabs in this dialog box, shown in Figures 9.15 and 9.16, are for reporting purposes. The first lets you specify the time periods involved, and the second lets you choose which of several optional graphs you want to produce. I typically ask for the two checked here.

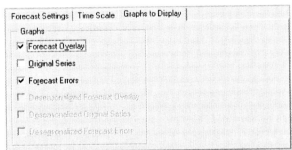

**Figure 9.15**

**Time Scale
Tab in
Forecasting
Dialog Box**

**Figure 9.16**

**Graphs to
Display Tab
in
Forecasting
Dialog Box**

The output from all StatTools forecasting procedures consists of a table of forecasts and forecast errors, any optional graphs you request, and a table of summary measures of the forecast errors. The table of forecasts and forecast errors (with many intermediate rows hidden) appears in Figure 9.17. The dotted lines toward the bottom indicate where the holdout and future periods begin. Because there are no observed sales for the future period, there can be no forecast errors for this period. Toward the top, each forecast is the average of the 6 sales just above it, which explains why there are no forecasts for the first 6 weeks. As a technical note, StatTools calculates future forecasts as averages of observed sales and previous forecasts (when observed sales are missing).

Figure 9.17

*Forecasts and Forecast Errors*

| Forecasting Data | Sales | Forecast | Error |
|---|---|---|---|
| 1 | 1526 | | |
| 2 | 1929 | | |
| 3 | 1704 | | |
| 4 | 1423 | | |
| 5 | 1430 | | |
| 6 | 1410 | | |
| 7 | 1478 | 1570.333 | -92.333 |
| 8 | 1698 | 1562.333 | 135.667 |
| 9 | 2223 | 1523.833 | 699.167 |
| 89 | 1517 | 2032.667 | -515.667 |
| 90 | 1378 | 1978.500 | -600.500 |
| 91 | 1448 | 1841.833 | -393.833 |
| 92 | 2196 | 1737.500 | 458.500 |
| 93 | 2053 | 1796.500 | 256.500 |
| 94 | 2170 | 1703.500 | 466.500 |
| 95 | 1755 | 1793.667 | -38.667 |
| 96 | 2056 | 1839.778 | 216.222 |
| 97 | 2152 | 1916.741 | 235.259 |
| 98 | 1069 | 1994.864 | -925.864 |
| 99 | 1306 | 1961.342 | -655.342 |
| 100 | 1302 | 1946.065 | -644.065 |
| 101 | 2361 | 1908.743 | 452.257 |
| 102 | 1658 | 1927.922 | -269.922 |
| 103 | 1903 | 1942.613 | -39.613 |
| 104 | 1702 | 1946.925 | -244.925 |
| 105 | | 1938.935 | |
| 106 | | 1935.200 | |
| 107 | | 1933.390 | |
| 108 | | 1937.497 | |
| 109 | | 1939.093 | |

The graph of the forecast series superimposed on the original series appears in Figure 9.18. The forecasts track the general movement of the series quite well, but the forecast series is much smoother, with no attempt to track every zigzag. Also, the future forecasts extending to the right are basically flat.

Figure 9.18

Forecast
Series
Superimposed
on Original
Series

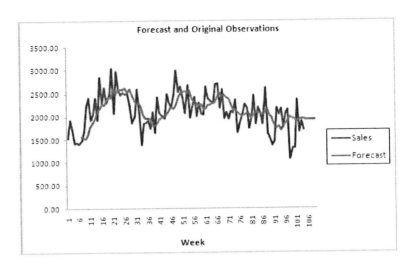

The series of forecast errors and the summary measures of the forecast errors are shown in Figures 9.19 and 9.20. Of course, you always want the forecast errors to be small in magnitude, but you also want the series of forecast errors to be a patternless series. If it had a pattern, it would be amenable to *further* forecasting. The series in Figure 9.19 appears to have this property, with no obvious patterns. Finally, the summary measures in Figure 9.20 indicate that the typical errors in the non-holdout period are about $275, which translates to about 13% of sales values. However, the forecast errors for the holdout period are quite a bit larger. This could be bad luck, or it could be a sign that the moving averages method with a span of 6 is not likely to produce accurate *future* forecasts for this series.

*Figure 9.19*

*Series of
Forecast
Errors*

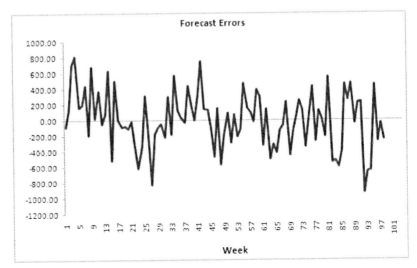

---

**Figure 9.20**

**Summary Measures of Forecast Errors**

| Forecasting Constant | | |
|---|---|---|
| Span | 6 | |
| | | |
| | Estimation | Holdouts |
| Moving Averages | Period | Period |
| Mean Abs Err | 275.20 | 372.21 |
| Root Mean Sq Err | 345.37 | 463.04 |
| Mean Abs Per% Err | 13.06% | 26.18% |

## Simple Exponential Smoothing

Exponential smoothing methods have the same basic goal as moving average methods: to smooth the series by taking averages of previous observations. However, exponential smoothing methods are more general. First, they forecast by taking *weighted* averages of previous observations, with more weight put on recent observations. Second, there are a variety of exponential smoothing methods available, depending on the nature of the series. If the series has no obvious trend or seasonality, then the method discussed here, **simple exponential smoothing**, is appropriate. If there is trend and/or seasonality, the methods discussed later in this chapter are appropriate.

All exponential smoothing methods employ one of more smoothing constants. A **smoothing constant** is a number between 0 and 1 that controls the amount weight put on recent observations versus observations in the distant past, and this in turn controls the amount of smoothing. The closer a smoothing constant is to 0, the more weight observations in the distant past receive, and the smoother the forecast series is. In this sense, a *small* smoothing constant is analogous to a *large* span for moving averages. For simple exponential smoothing, there is a single smoothing constant, usually labeled $\alpha$ (alpha). StatTools allows you to choose this smoothing constant. Alternatively, you can check an **Optimize Parameters** box, in which case StatTools finds the smoothing constant that minimizes the RMSE.

Simple exponential smoothing actually estimates a **level** of the series at each period. This level can be interpreted as the value of the series you would expect if it were not for noise. The procedure estimates this level as a weighted average of the previous level and the most recent observation, using the smoothing constant for weighting. It then forecasts that all future observations will equal this level, reasoning that the series isn't really going anywhere.

To illustrate simple exponential smoothing, consider the same hardware sales series that was used to illustrate moving averages. Because this series has no obvious trend or seasonality, it is a good candidate for simple exponential smoothing. To employ the method, select **Forecast** from the **Time Series & Forecasting** dropdown and fill out the same dialog box as with moving averages. (See Figure 9.21.) In fact, the only change is the forecasting method. You now select the second method and choose a smoothing constant. Actually, if you check the Optimize Parameters box, as I did here, the smoothing constant you select is not important; StatTools reports only the *optimal* smoothing constant.

Figure 9.21

Forecasting
Dialog Box
for Simple
Exponential
Smoothing

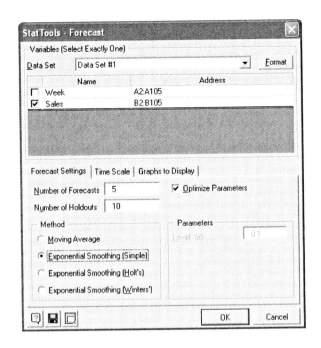

The exponential smoothing output is very similar to moving averages output. The forecasts and forecast errors are shown in Figure 9.22. As mentioned earlier, each forecast is a weighted average of a sales value and a level, with the weights determined by the smoothing constant. The forecasting formula is not shown here, but it is instructive to view the formulas that StatTools enters in the Level and Forecast columns to see how exponential smoothing works. Note the forecasts for the holdout and future periods are constant. This always occurs with simple exponential smoothing, again because the basic assumption of simple exponential smoothing is that the series is really not going anywhere.

Figure 9.22

Forecasts
and
Forecast
Errors

| Forecasting Data | Sales | Level | Forecast | Error |
|---|---|---|---|---|
| 1 | 1526 | 1526 | | |
| 2 | 1929 | 1669.43 | 1526.00 | 403.00 |
| 3 | 1704 | 1681.73 | 1669.43 | 34.57 |
| 4 | 1423 | 1589.65 | 1681.73 | -258.73 |
| 5 | 1430 | 1532.83 | 1589.65 | -159.65 |
| 6 | 1410 | 1489.12 | 1532.83 | -122.83 |
| 7 | 1478 | 1485.16 | 1489.12 | -11.12 |
| 8 | 1698 | 1560.91 | 1485.16 | 212.84 |
| 9 | 2223 | 1796.55 | 1560.91 | 662.09 |
| 89 | 1517 | 1833.52 | 2008.42 | -491.42 |
| 90 | 1378 | 1671.40 | 1833.52 | -455.52 |
| 91 | 1448 | 1591.89 | 1671.40 | -223.40 |
| 92 | 2196 | 1806.89 | 1591.89 | 604.11 |
| 93 | 2053 | 1894.48 | 1806.89 | 246.11 |
| 94 | 2170 | 1992.54 | 1894.48 | 275.52 |
| 95 | 1755 | | 1992.54 | -237.54 |
| 96 | 2056 | | 1992.54 | 63.46 |
| 97 | 2152 | | 1992.54 | 159.46 |
| 98 | 1069 | | 1992.54 | -923.54 |
| 99 | 1306 | | 1992.54 | -686.54 |
| 100 | 1302 | | 1992.54 | -690.54 |
| 101 | 2361 | | 1992.54 | 368.46 |
| 102 | 1658 | | 1992.54 | -334.54 |
| 103 | 1903 | | 1992.54 | -89.54 |
| 104 | 1702 | | 1992.54 | -290.54 |
| 105 | | | 1992.54 | |
| 106 | | | 1992.54 | |
| 107 | | | 1992.54 | |
| 108 | | | 1992.54 | |
| 109 | | | 1992.54 | |

The forecast series superimposed on the original series appears in Figure 9.23. As with moving averages, the forecast series is smoother than the original series, but it tracks the general ups and downs quite well. The graph of the series of forecast errors (not shown here but available from StatTools) is basically the same as for moving averages in that it exhibits no obvious patterns.

**Figure 9.23**

**Forecast Series Superimposed on Original Series**

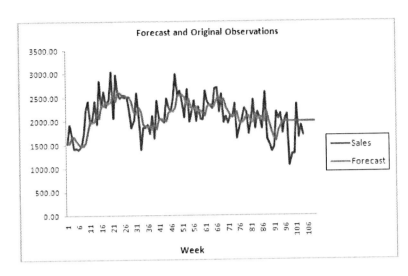

At the top of the output, StatTools lists the smoothing constant (the optimal one in this case) and a table of summary measures of forecasting errors. (See Figure 9.24.) Analysts generally favor smoothing constants in the 0.1 to 0.2 range, but there is nothing sacred about this range. For these data, the value 0.356 evidently works best in terms of minimizing RMSE. Note that all of the StatTools outputs are linked to this smoothing constant by means of formulas. Therefore, if you want to try another smoothing constant, you can simply enter another value in the smoothing constant cell.

**Figure 9.24**

**Optimal Smoothing Constant and Summary Measures of Forecast Errors**

| Forecasting Constant (Optimized) | | |
|---|---|---|
| Level (Alpha) | | 0.356 |
| | Estimation | Holdouts |
| Simple Exponential | Period | Period |
| Mean Abs Err | 258.24 | 384.42 |
| Root Mean Sq Err | 332.02 | 471.92 |
| Mean Abs Per% Err | 12.34% | 27.36% |

## Holt's Method for Trend

If a series has an obvious upward or downward trend, the forecasts from simple exponential smoothing will tend to lag behind the trend. The version of exponential smoothing discussed here, **Holt's method**, is much better able to track a trend. This method has two smoothing constants, one for estimating the level (defined as before), and one for estimating the trend (the change from one period to the next). These are usually labeled α and β (beta). They are used, along with two equations for updating level and trend, to produce the forecasts.

To illustrate Holt's method, consider the quarterly sales (in millions of dollars) of a computer chip manufacturer in Figure 9.25. (The data actually extend through the end of year 2008. See the file **Chip Sales.xlsx** for the full data set.) The time series graph of sales, shown in Figure 9.26, indicates a clear upward trend, one that simple exponential smoothing would not track well.

*Figure 9.25*

*Quarterly Chip Sales*

| | A | B |
|---|---|---|
| 1 | Quarter | Sales |
| 2 | Q1-94 | 280.05 |
| 3 | Q2-94 | 305.18 |
| 4 | Q3-94 | 324.14 |
| 5 | Q4-94 | 355.64 |
| 6 | Q1-95 | 394.53 |
| 7 | Q2-95 | 438.96 |
| 8 | Q3-95 | 501.13 |
| 9 | Q4-95 | 572.49 |
| 10 | Q1-96 | 635.81 |
| 11 | Q2-96 | 726.68 |

*Figure 9.26*

*Time Series Graph of Chip Sales*

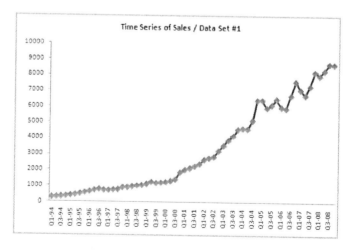

To run Holt's method, select **Forecast** from the **Time Series & Forecasting** dropdown and fill in the forecasting dialog box as in Figures 9.27 and 9.28. In this case (for variety), I have chosen not to have a holdout period, but I have again asked StatTools to optimize the two smoothing constants. For labeling purposes, I specify that the data are quarterly and begin with quarter 1 of 1994.

**Figure 9.27**

**Forecasting Dialog Box for Holt's Method**

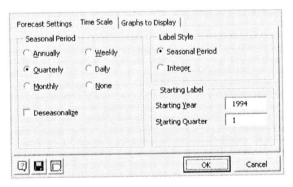

**Figure 9.28**

**Time Scale Tab for Specifying Time Period**

The forecasts and forecast errors appear in Figure 9.29 (with many intermediate rows hidden). Note that the level continues to increase, whereas the estimate of trend remains at the same value throughout. This value is the estimated amount sales will increase each quarter. To see how the forecasts work, each *future* forecast starts with the ending level, 8702, and adds a multiple of the ending trend, 140.366, for each successive quarter. For example, the forecast for Q2–2009 is 8702.000+2(140.366).

*Figure 9.29*

*Forecasts
and
Forecast
Errors*

| Forecasting Data | Sales | Level | Trend | Forecast | Error |
|---|---|---|---|---|---|
| Q1-1994 | 280.0540 | 280.05 | 140.37 | | |
| Q2-1994 | 305.1780 | 305.18 | 140.37 | 420.42 | -115.24 |
| Q3-1994 | 324.1370 | 324.14 | 140.37 | 445.54 | -121.41 |
| Q4-1994 | 355.6420 | 355.64 | 140.37 | 464.50 | -108.86 |
| Q1-1995 | 394.5330 | 394.53 | 140.37 | 496.01 | -101.47 |
| Q2-1995 | 438.9560 | 438.96 | 140.37 | 534.90 | -95.94 |
| Q3-1995 | 501.1280 | 501.13 | 140.37 | 579.32 | -78.19 |
| Q4-1995 | 572.4880 | 572.49 | 140.37 | 641.49 | -69.01 |
| Q1-1996 | 635.8070 | 635.81 | 140.37 | 712.85 | -77.05 |
| Q2-1996 | 726.6830 | 726.68 | 140.37 | 776.17 | -49.49 |
| Q2-2008 | 8300.0000 | 8300.00 | 140.37 | 8133.37 | 166.63 |
| Q3-2008 | 8731.0000 | 8731.00 | 140.37 | 8440.37 | 290.63 |
| Q4-2008 | 8702.0000 | 8702.00 | 140.37 | 8871.37 | -169.37 |
| Q1-2009 | | | | 8842.37 | |
| Q2-2009 | | | | 8982.73 | |
| Q3-2009 | | | | 9123.10 | |
| Q4-2009 | | | | 9263.46 | |
| Q1-2010 | | | | 9403.83 | |
| Q2-2010 | | | | 9544.19 | |
| Q3-2010 | | | | 9684.56 | |
| Q4-2010 | | | | 9824.93 | |

Figure 9.30 indicates how Holt's method tracks the upward trend and projects this trend into the future. However, the graph of the forecast errors in Figure 9.31 indicates that the bumpiness in the series in the last few years is more difficult to track. This raises concerns about the ability of the method to forecast the *future* years accurately.

*Figure 9.30*

*Forecast
Series
Superimposed
on Original
Series*

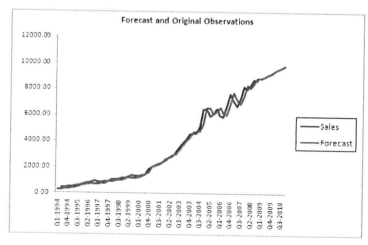

**Figure 9.31**

**Series of
Forecast
Errors**

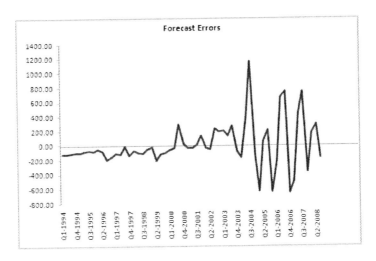

The optimal smoothing constants, shown in Figure 9.32, are interesting. The smoothing constant of 1 for level means that the method reacts right away to every observed change in level, whereas the smoothing constant of 0 for trend means that the method never changes its initial estimate of trend. Recall that these values are the ones that optimize RMSE. However, there is no guarantee that they are really *best*, in the sense of guaranteeing the most accurate *future* forecasts. If you want to try other values for these constants, you can do so easily. Because all of the StatTools outputs are linked by formulas to these smoothing constant cells, they update automatically when you change the smoothing constants.

**Figure 9.32**

**Optimal
Smoothing
Constants
and
Summary
Measures
of Forecast
Errors**

| Forecasting Constants (Optimized) | |
|---|---|
| Level (Alpha) | 1.000 |
| Trend (Beta) | 0.000 |
| | |
| Holt's Exponential | |
| Mean Abs Err | 212.01 |
| Root Mean Sq Err | 311.93 |
| Mean Abs Per% Err | 9.51% |

## Forecasting Seasonality

None of the forecasting methods discussed to this point is capable of dealing with the seasonal patterns evident in many time series. StatTools provides two alternative methods for dealing with seasonality. The first is another version of exponential smoothing, **Winters' method**. The second is a more roundabout approach, where the data are first **deseasonalized** to remove the seasonal pattern. Then any forecasting method, such as Holt's method or moving averages, can be used to forecast the deseasonalized series, and finally, the deseasonalized forecasts are **reseasonalized** to obtain forecasts for the original series.

I first discuss Winters' exponential smoothing method. It builds on Holt's method, again using smoothing constants $\alpha$ and $\beta$ for level and trend, but it also uses a third smoothing constant, generally denoted $\gamma$ (gamma), for seasonality. This smoothing constant controls the updating of a whole year's worth of **seasonal indexes**. For example, the data are quarterly and the seasonal indexes for quarters 1 and 2 are 0.8 and 1.1, this means that quarter 1 observations are typically about 20% below the average of all observations, whereas quarter 2 observations are typically about 10% above the average of all observations. Winters' method uses three equations, together with the three smoothing constants, to update the level, the trend, and the seasonal indexes.

To illustrate Winters' method, consider the quarterly data in Figure 9.33 on a company's soft drink sales (in thousands of dollars). (The data actually extend through the year 2008. The full data set is in the file **Soft Drink Sales.xlsx**.) The time series graph of sales, shown in Figure 9.34, indicates a clear pattern: an upward trend and a regular seasonal pattern, with higher sales in quarters 2 and 3 and lower sales in quarters 1 and 4. Simple exponential smoothing and Holt's method would miss this seasonal pattern entirely.

*Figure 9.33*

*Soft Drink Sales*

|   | A | B |
|---|---|---|
| 1 | Quarter | Sales |
| 2 | Q1-94 | 1734.83 |
| 3 | Q2-94 | 2244.96 |
| 4 | Q3-94 | 2533.80 |
| 5 | Q4-94 | 2154.96 |
| 6 | Q1-95 | 1547.82 |
| 7 | Q2-95 | 2104.41 |
| 8 | Q3-95 | 2014.36 |
| 9 | Q4-95 | 1991.75 |
| 10 | Q1-96 | 1869.05 |
| 11 | Q2-96 | 2313.63 |

Figure 9.34

Time Series
Graph of
Soft Drink
Sales

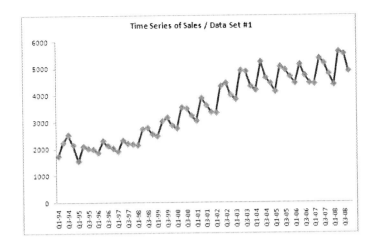

To use Winters' method, fill in the forecasting dialog box as in Figure 9.35. The only difference from Holt's method is that there is now a third smoothing constant. Note that when you select Winters' method in this dialog box, the Deseasonalize option in the Time Scale tab (not shown here) is disabled. There is a good reason for this. When you use Winters' method, it takes care of seasonality explicitly, so there is no reason to deseasonalize first.

Figure 9.35

Forecasting
Dialog Box
for Winters'
Method

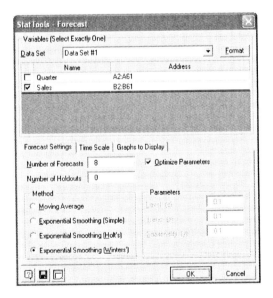

The forecast output shown in Figure 9.36 is also similar to Holt's output. The only difference is that there is now a Season column for the seasonal indexes. In this example, the seasonal indexes for quarters 1 and 4 are less than 1, and those for quarters 2 and 3 are greater than 1. To calculate future forecasts, StatTools proceeds exactly as in Holt's method, adding multiples of the final estimate of trend to the final estimate of level. But it then multiplies this sum by the relevant seasonal index to obtain the forecast. For example, the forecast for Q2–2009 is 1.10[5109.00+2(52.44)].

*Figure 9.36*

*Forecasts and Forecast Errors*

| Forecasting Data | Sales | Level | Trend | Season | Forecast | Error |
|---|---|---|---|---|---|---|
| Q1-1994 | 1734.8270 | 1954.17 | 52.44 | 0.89 | | |
| Q2-1994 | 2244.9610 | 2039.64 | 52.44 | 1.10 | 2202.43 | 42.53 |
| Q3-1994 | 2533.8050 | 2359.06 | 52.44 | 1.05 | 2203.81 | 329.99 |
| Q4-1994 | 2154.9630 | 2266.90 | 52.44 | 0.96 | 2318.05 | -163.09 |
| Q1-1995 | 1547.8190 | 1828.58 | 52.44 | 0.89 | 2059.01 | -511.19 |
| Q2-1995 | 2104.4120 | 1911.95 | 52.44 | 1.10 | 2064.59 | 39.82 |
| Q3-1995 | 2014.3630 | 1919.94 | 52.44 | 1.05 | 2069.30 | -54.94 |
| Q4-1995 | 1991.7470 | 2057.32 | 52.44 | 0.96 | 1895.94 | 95.80 |
| Q1-2008 | 4391.0000 | 4961.22 | 52.44 | 0.89 | 4481.38 | -90.38 |
| Q2-2008 | 5621.0000 | 5105.34 | 52.44 | 1.10 | 5602.94 | 118.06 |
| Q3-2008 | 5543.0000 | 5246.57 | 52.44 | 1.05 | 5433.26 | 109.74 |
| Q4-2008 | 4903.0000 | 5129.96 | 52.44 | 0.96 | 5093.66 | -190.66 |
| Q1-2009 | | | | | 4600.71 | |
| Q2-2009 | | | | | 5745.70 | |
| Q3-2009 | | | | | 5569.68 | |
| Q4-2009 | | | | | 5132.80 | |
| Q1-2010 | | | | | 4786.93 | |
| Q2-2010 | | | | | 5975.94 | |
| Q3-2010 | | | | | 5790.65 | |
| Q4-2010 | | | | | 5334.44 | |

The graph in Figure 9.37 indicates how Winters' method tracks the trend and the seasonal pattern and projects these into the future. The output in Figure 9.38 shows that these accurate forecasts (off by only about 3.56%) are produced by a large smoothing constant for level and negligible smoothing constants for trend and seasonality. Again, however, you can try other smoothing constants if you like.

*Figure 9.37*

*Forecast Series Superimposed on Original Series*

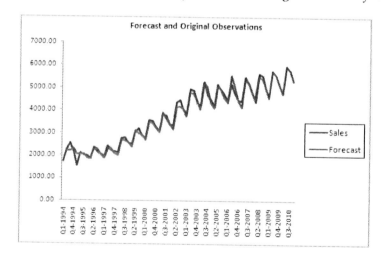

**Figure 9.38**

**Optimal Smoothing Constants and Summary Measures of Forecast Errors**

| Forecasting Constants (Optimized) | |
|---|---|
| Level (Alpha) | 0.852 |
| Trend (Beta) | 0.000 |
| Season (Gamma) | 0.000 |
| | |
| Winters' Exponential | |
| Mean Abs Err | 114.36 |
| Root Mean Sq Err | 156.96 |
| Mean Abs Per% Err | 3.56% |

A second method for dealing with seasonality is to deseasonalize the data first and then use any forecasting method (except Winters' method, which wouldn't make sense) to forecast the deseasonalized data. StatTools first uses a **ratio to centered moving averages** scheme to estimate seasonal indexes. Suppose that it estimates the seasonal index for quarter 1 to be 0.89. Then to deseasonalize, it *divides* each quarter 1 observation by 0.89. This division magnifies quarters with low values and shrinks quarters with high values, thereby removing the seasonal pattern.

To illustrate this method with the soft drink sales series, note again that except for the seasonal pattern in this series, sales are trending upward. Therefore, the deseasonalized series will, aside from noise, be a fairly smooth upward trend, so it makes sense to estimate it by Holt's method. To use this approach, choose Holt's method in the forecasting dialog box and check the Deseasonalize option in the Time Scale tab, as in Figure 9.39. When you check this option, the Graphs to Display tab in Figure 9.40 allows you to select three extra graphs. The first three options are for the original data, and the three extra options are for the deseasonalized data.

*Figure 9.39*

*Forecasting
Dialog Box with
Deseasonalizing
Method*

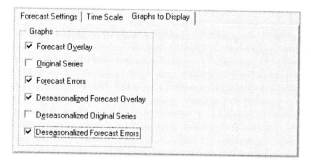

*Figure 9.40*

*Graph Options
with
Deseasonalizing
Method*

The forecast output shown in Figure 9.41 provides a lot of information. The seasonal indexes in the third column are used to obtain the deseasonalized series in the fourth column, and Holt's method is then used to forecast this series, with the results in the Deseason columns. Finally, the seasonal indexes are used again (this time, using multiplication, not division) to obtain the reseasonalized forecasts and forecast errors in the last two columns.

*Figure 9.41*

*Forecasts and Forecast Errors*

| Forecasting Data | Sales | Season Index | Deseason Sales | Deseason Level | Deseason Trend | Deseason Forecast | Deseason Errors | Season Forecast | Season Errors |
|---|---|---|---|---|---|---|---|---|---|
| Q1-1994 | 1734.8270 | 0.89 | 1954.17 | 1954.17 | 52.44 | | | 2202.43 | 42.53 |
| Q2-1994 | 2244.9610 | 1.10 | 2045.36 | 2039.55 | 52.44 | 2006.61 | 38.75 | 2203.72 | 330.08 |
| Q3-1994 | 2533.8050 | 1.05 | 2405.34 | 2368.34 | 52.44 | 2091.99 | 313.35 | 2317.35 | -162.39 |
| Q4-1994 | 2154.9630 | 0.96 | 2241.84 | 2267.18 | 52.44 | 2410.78 | -168.94 | 2059.26 | -511.44 |
| Q1-1995 | 1647.8190 | 0.89 | 1743.52 | 1829.94 | 52.44 | 2319.62 | -576.10 | 2066.07 | 38.34 |
| Q2-1995 | 2104.4120 | 1.10 | 1917.31 | 1912.07 | 52.44 | 1882.38 | 34.93 | 2069.43 | -55.07 |
| Q3-1995 | 2014.3630 | 1.05 | 1912.23 | 1920.07 | 52.44 | 1964.51 | -52.28 | 1896.07 | 95.67 |
| Q4-1995 | 1991.7470 | 0.96 | 2072.04 | 2057.11 | 52.44 | 1972.51 | 99.53 | 4481.36 | -90.38 |
| Q1-2008 | 4391.0000 | 0.89 | 4946.18 | 4961.45 | 52.44 | 5047.99 | -101.81 | 5603.19 | 117.81 |
| Q2-2008 | 5621.0000 | 1.10 | 5121.23 | 5105.13 | 52.44 | 5013.89 | 107.34 | 5433.03 | 109.97 |
| Q3-2008 | 5543.0000 | 1.05 | 5261.96 | 5246.30 | 52.44 | 5157.57 | 104.39 | 5093.40 | -190.40 |
| Q4-2008 | 4903.0000 | 0.96 | 5100.66 | 5130.38 | 52.44 | 5298.74 | -198.08 | | |
| Q1-2009 | | 0.89 | | | | 5182.82 | | 4601.07 | |
| Q2-2009 | | 1.10 | | | | 5235.26 | | 5746.16 | |
| Q3-2009 | | 1.05 | | | | 5287.70 | | 5570.11 | |
| Q4-2009 | | 0.96 | | | | 5340.14 | | 5133.20 | |
| Q1-2010 | | 0.89 | | | | 5392.58 | | 4787.30 | |
| Q2-2010 | | 1.10 | | | | 5445.03 | | 5976.39 | |
| Q3-2010 | | 1.05 | | | | 5497.47 | | 5791.08 | |
| Q4-2010 | | 0.96 | | | | 5549.91 | | 5334.83 | |

The reseasonalized forecasts superimposed on the original data appear in Figure 9.42. This graph is very similar to the one from Winters' method. For comparison, StatTools also graphs the deseasonalized forecasts superimposed on the deseasonalized series, as shown in Figure 9.43. This graph contains none of the seasonality, only the upward trend. Essentially, this method uses two steps. It first forecasts the upward trend, using any applicable method, such as Holt's method. Then it applies seasonal indexes to the results.

*Figure 9.42*

*Forecast Series Overlaid on Original Series*

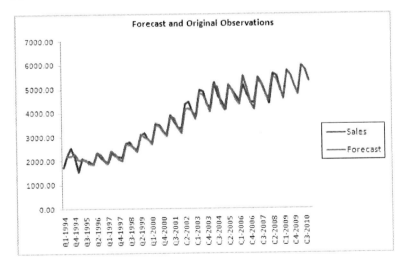

Figure 9.43

Deseasonlized
Forecast Series
Superimposed
on
Deseasonalized
Series

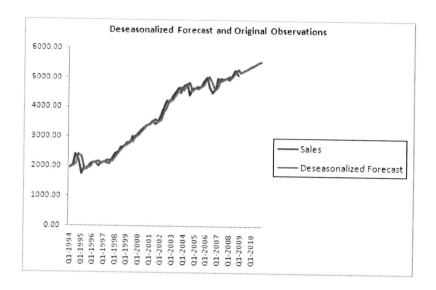

By comparing the left-hand summary measures in Figure 9.44 from this method to the summary measures in Figure 9.38 from Winters' method, it is apparent the two approaches give very similar results. This is not at all uncommon.

**Figure 9.44**

*Optimal
Smoothing
Constants
and
Summary
Measures
of Forecast
Errors*

| Forecasting Constants (Optimized) | | |
|---|---|---|
| Level (Alpha) | 0.850 | |
| Trend (Beta) | 0.000 | |

| Holt's Exponential | | Deseason Estimate |
|---|---|---|
| Mean Abs Err | 114.30 | 114.10 |
| Root Mean Sq Err | 156.96 | 158.03 |
| Mean Abs Per% Err | 3.56% | 3.56% |

**Notes**

- Once a time series has been deseasonalized, *any* reasonable forecasting method, not just Holt's method, can be used to forecast the deseasonalized series. Then it is just a matter of multiplying by the seasonal indexes to obtain forecasts of the original series.

# Chapter 10: Quality Control

## 10.1 Introduction

*Quality
Control
Icon*

To compete in today's business world, companies must produce high-quality goods and provide high-quality service. Many statistical tools have been developed to measure and track quality, both for manufacturing and service organizations. Control charts are among the most prominent of these tools. These charts, which are typically monitored continuously in real time, allow a company to see whether a process remains **in control**. If a chart suddenly indicates an **out-of-control** condition, the company can immediately react and hopefully fix the problem quickly. There are a number of different types of control charts available, depending on the type of data being observed, and StatTools implements the most common types. Although these types differ in their details, their common purpose is to monitor a process so that out-of-control conditions can be spotted and fixed quickly.

## 10.2 X-Bar Charts and R Charts

Probably the most common types of control charts are **X-bar charts** and **R charts**. These charts, usually shown together as a pair, are relevant for measurements on a continuous scale. The typical situation is that a company makes several observations on a process at regular points in time. The purpose of the charts is to check whether the average and variability of the process remain stable, without any unexpected behavior.

As an example, consider a manufacturing process that produces 12-ounce cans of soda. To ensure that the contents of the cans stays near 12 ounces, measurements are made on 5 randomly selected soda cans every 15 minutes. The data are stored as in Figure 10.1. (Actually, there are 70 samples; only the first 10 are shown. The full data set is in the file **Soda Cans.xlsx**.) Each sample (row) contains the 5 observations made at approximately the same time during a 15-minute period.

Figure 10.1

Soda Can
Data

| | A | B | C | D | E | F |
|---|---|---|---|---|---|---|
| 1 | Sample | Obs1 | Obs2 | Obs3 | Obs4 | Obs5 |
| 2 | 1 | 11.991 | 12.001 | 12.176 | 12.004 | 12.030 |
| 3 | 2 | 12.065 | 12.018 | 12.223 | 11.955 | 11.959 |
| 4 | 3 | 11.946 | 11.980 | 12.089 | 12.125 | 12.111 |
| 5 | 4 | 12.011 | 12.069 | 12.065 | 12.155 | 12.197 |
| 6 | 5 | 11.783 | 12.140 | 12.008 | 12.076 | 12.044 |
| 7 | 6 | 11.962 | 12.132 | 12.149 | 11.991 | 12.128 |
| 8 | 7 | 12.163 | 11.961 | 11.932 | 12.115 | 11.870 |
| 9 | 8 | 12.053 | 12.053 | 11.889 | 11.975 | 12.037 |
| 10 | 9 | 12.108 | 11.942 | 12.102 | 11.967 | 12.056 |
| 11 | 10 | 11.869 | 12.056 | 12.109 | 12.079 | 12.235 |

For each sample, the 5 observations are averaged to get an X-bar value. This provides an estimate of the average fill amount at that time. Also, the smallest of the 5 observations is subtracted from the largest to obtain an R value (R for range). This provides an estimate of the amount of variability in the process at that time. The control charts then plot the series of X-bar values and the series of R values so that it is possible to check for unusual conditions.

To create these control charts with StatTools, select **X/R Charts** from the **Quality Control** dropdown. This brings up the dialog box in Figure 10.2. Because of the many ways these charts are used in real applications, this dialog box provides a number of options. In the top dropdown list, you can request both X-bar and R charts (the usual practice, selected here) or either one or the other.

Figure 10.2

Dialog Box
for X-Bar
and R
Charts

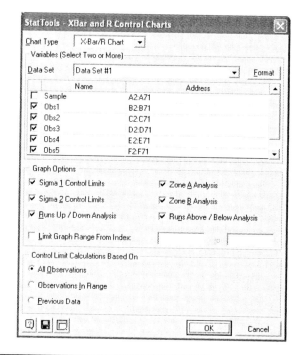

By default, the only out-of-control condition these control charts check for is whether any points are beyond **upper and lower control limits**, defined as plus or minus 3 standard deviations from a **centerline**. The middle Graph Options section in the dialog box allows you to request additional checks, discussed below. It also lets you limit the samples graphed. (By default, all samples in the data set are graphed.) For example, an alternative way of filling in this middle section appears in Figure 10.3.

**Figure 10.3**

*Alternative Graph Options*

The control charts are based on centerlines and 3-standard deviation control limits. By default (as shown in Figure 10.2), these centerlines and control limits are based on *all* of the samples in the data set. However, you can change this through the settings in the bottom section of the dialog box. In Figure 10.4, I have changed the settings so that the centerline and control limits are based only on the first 40 samples. This might be appropriate, say, if you already know the process is in control during this period, and you want to see if it stays in control, at the same levels, for the remaining periods. Another option appears in Figure 10.5. Here I have indicated that the centerline and control limits should be based on previous data, where there were 5 observations per sample, with the averages shown. Again, StatTools provides this flexibility so that the control charts can be used in the ways they are actually used in real applications.

**Figure 10.4**

*Alternative Settings for Control Limit Calculations*

| Control Limit Calculations Based On | | |
| --- | --- | --- |
| ○ All Observations | Start Index | 1 |
| ● Observations In Range | Stop Index | 40 |
| ○ Previous Data | | |

**Figure 10.5**

*Other Alternative Settings for Control Limit Calculations*

| Control Limit Calculations Based On | | |
| --- | --- | --- |
| ○ All Observations | Subsample Size | 5 |
| ○ Observations In Range | Average R | 0.25 |
| ● Previous Data | Average X-Bar | 12.03 |

The StatTools output (based on the settings in Figure 10.2) consists of an X-bar chart, an R chart, and the calculated data (not shown here) used as the basis for the charts. Typically, it is a good idea to examine the R chart first. It appears in Figure 10.6. This chart shows how the variability in the samples changes through time. You are looking for unusual points or patterns. An unusual point is one the lies beyond the dotted control limit lines. There are no such points here. In addition, if you check the Runs options in the dialog box, you are warned about unusual runs of sufficient length up or down or on either side of the centerline. Either of these reflects suspicious behavior that might warrant further investigation. In this example, there was one rather long run below the centerline, which StatTools colors green. Except for this run, however, the R chart indicates that the variability of the process is in control.

**Figure 10.6**

**R Chart**

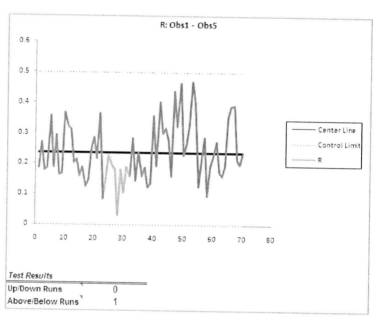

Assuming that the R chart shows no problems, it then makes sense to examine the X-bar chart in Figure 10.7. This is a time series chart of the X-bars from the samples. As with the R chart, you are always looking for points beyond the 3-standard deviation control limits, none of which are present in this data set. In addition, depending on which other options are requested in the dialog box, StatTools can make the following checks:

1) Runs of at least 8 consecutive increases or decreases

2) Runs of at least 8 consecutive points above or below the centerline

3) 2 out of 3 consecutive points beyond **zone A**, defined as the range within 2 standard deviations of the centerline

4) 4 out of 5 consecutive points beyond **zone B**, defined as the range within 1 standard deviation of the centerline

Each of these is an "unusual" sequence worthy of further investigation. If StatTools finds any of these, it colors or marks that part of the sequence. (Note that all of these checks are available for the X-bar chart, but only the first two checks are available for the R chart. This is standard practice.) For this particular X-bar chart, there is one long run below the centerline and two zone B violations, both toward the end of the series, that might warrant further investigation.

**Figure 10.7**

**X-Bar Chart**

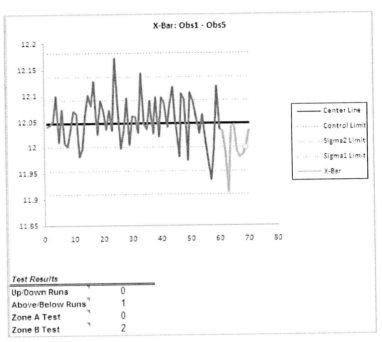

**Notes**

- If you look at Figure 10.7 carefully and read the cell comment for the zone B test, you will probably be puzzled why there are 2 zone B violations, even though only one point is circled as such. It is *not* a bug in StatTools. StatTools looks for cases where 4 out of 5 consecutive points are beyond zone B, and it circles the 4th of these. In this case, points 66–69 are beyond zone B, so the sequence 65–69 qualifies, as does the sequence 66–70. Since point 69 is the 4th point beyond zone B in each of these sequences, it is essentially circled twice. This accounts for the apparent inconsistency.

# 10.3 P Charts

The X-bar and R charts from the previous section are applicable for **measurement data**, such as weights or lengths. The charts in this section, **P charts**, are used for **attribute data**, where each item either conforms or does not conform to given specifications. Essentially, attribute data is all or nothing. Either an item conforms to specifications or it doesn't.

A typical data set appears in Figure 10.8. (There are actually data for 25 hours. The full data set is in the file **Sound Chips 1.xlsx**.) During each hour, a process produces a batch of 75 sound chips. The third column lists the numbers that do not conform to specifications. This is the typical setup expected by StatTools for P charts. However, several variations are possible: (1) a sample size variable (as in the middle column) is not required if the sample sizes are equal; (2) if there is a sample size variable, the sample sizes do not have to be equal; and (3) instead of listing the *numbers* of nonconforming items, the *fractions* of nonconforming items can be listed.

*Figure 10.8*

*Sound Chip Data with Common Sample Size*

| | A | B | C |
|---|---|---|---|
| 1 | Hour | SampleSize | Nonconforming |
| 2 | 1 | 75 | 17 |
| 3 | 2 | 75 | 18 |
| 4 | 3 | 75 | 18 |
| 5 | 4 | 75 | 16 |
| 6 | 5 | 75 | 20 |
| 7 | 6 | 75 | 22 |
| 8 | 7 | 75 | 24 |
| 9 | 8 | 75 | 19 |
| 10 | 9 | 75 | 15 |
| 11 | 10 | 75 | 22 |

To create a P chart, select **P Chart** from the **Quality Control** dropdown and fill in the resulting dialog box as in Figure 10.9. Note that the "Val" variable chosen corresponds to the Input Data option—that is, it can contain counts of nonconforming items or fractions of nonconforming items. Also, the Use Size Variable option in the Sample Size section is enabled only if you specify a "Siz" variable above. For this particular data set, where there is a common sample size of 75 each hour, you could also fill in the top part of the dialog box as in Figure 10.10. Besides this, the other settings in the dialog box are equivalent to those for X-bar/R charts.

**Figure 10.9**

**Dialog Box for P Chart**

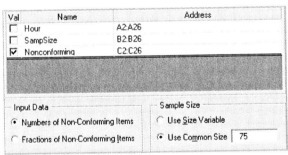

**Figure 10.10**

**Alternative Dialog Box Settings with Common Sample Size**

The resulting P chart appears in Figure 10.11. It is a time series chart of the fractions nonconforming. (*Fractions* are always graphed, regardless of the form of the input data.) This chart indicates that the process is well in control, with no points near the control limits and no up/down or above/below runs.

---

Figure 10.11

P Chart

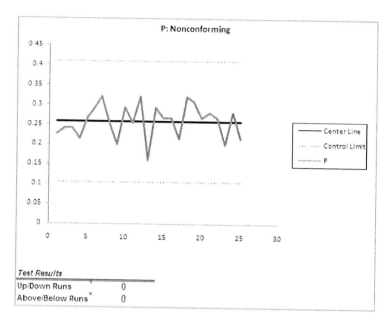

It is possible that the sample sizes are *not* constant from one hour to the next, as might be the case in a real manufacturing environment. Then the data could be as in Figure 10.12, where the SampSize variable is not constant. (Again, there are 25 hours in this data set. See the file **Sound Chips 2.xlsx**.) You still fill in the dialog box exactly as in Figure 10.9, but the resulting P chart, shown in Figure 10.13, now has wavy control limits, due to the unequal sample sizes. For this data set, no points are beyond the control limits, but there is one suspicious long run below the centerline.

**Figure 10.12**

*Sound Chip Data with Unequal Sample Sizes*

| | A | B | C |
|---|---|---|---|
| 1 | Hour | SampleSize | Nonconforming |
| 2 | 1 | 84 | 23 |
| 3 | 2 | 71 | 14 |
| 4 | 3 | 86 | 18 |
| 5 | 4 | 63 | 18 |
| 6 | 5 | 77 | 15 |
| 7 | 6 | 66 | 18 |
| 8 | 7 | 60 | 9 |
| 9 | 8 | 62 | 14 |
| 10 | 9 | 76 | 22 |
| 11 | 10 | 75 | 20 |

**Figure 10.13**

*P Chart with Unequal Sample Sizes*

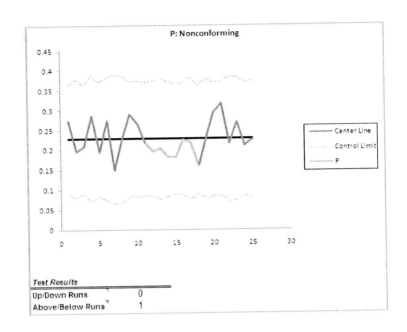

# 10.4 C Charts and U Charts

The control charts discussed to this point are probably the most commonly used types, but the two types discussed in this section, C charts and U charts, find many uses as well. A C chart is used to track defects in units of a *fixed* size, whereas a U chart is used to track defects in units of *varying* sizes.

For example, consider the data in Figure 10.14. (There are actually 50 units. The full data set is in the file **Paint Blemishes 1.xlsx**.) In this situation, metal plates, each of size 66 square feet, have been painted and then examined for blemishes. The numbers of blemishes are listed in the third column. The purpose of a C chart is to track these blemish counts through time.

*Figure 10.14*

*Defects in Units of a Fixed Size*

| | A | B | C |
|---|---|---|---|
| 1 | Unit | SqFt | Blemishes |
| 2 | 1 | 66 | 2 |
| 3 | 2 | 66 | 2 |
| 4 | 3 | 66 | 0 |
| 5 | 4 | 66 | 0 |
| 6 | 5 | 66 | 1 |
| 7 | 6 | 66 | 4 |
| 8 | 7 | 66 | 0 |
| 9 | 8 | 66 | 0 |
| 10 | 9 | 66 | 2 |
| 11 | 10 | 66 | 3 |

To create a C chart, select **C Chart** from the **Quality Control** dropdown and fill in the resulting dialog box in the usual way, as shown in Figure 10.15. The only variable selected is the variable that lists the blemish counts. This produces the C chart in Figure 10.16. Note that the upper control limit is farther from the centerline than the lower control limit at 0. This is because it makes no sense for counts to be negative. Therefore, the lower control limit often coincides with the horizontal axis. There are no out-of-control indications in this chart.

**Figure 10.15**

**Dialog Box for C Chart**

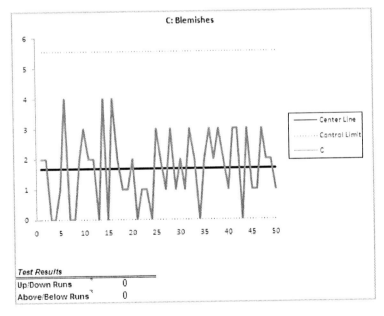

**Figure 10.16**

**C Chart**

If the metal plates are of varying square footages, as in Figure 10.17, then a U chart is appropriate. (There are again 50 units in this data set. See the file **Paint Blemishes 2.xlsx**.) Instead of tracking the *number* of blemishes on these plates, you now track the *rate* of blemishes per square foot, shown in the right-hand column. For example, the first rate is 5/73. The idea is that if the sizes of the plates vary widely, you would expect the numbers of blemishes to vary, but the rates should remain fairly constant.

**Figure 10.17**

*Defects in Units of Varying Sizes*

| | A | B | C | D |
|---|---|---|---|---|
| 1 | Unit | SqFt | Blemishes | Rate |
| 2 | 1 | 73 | 5 | 0.0685 |
| 3 | 2 | 70 | 4 | 0.0571 |
| 4 | 3 | 60 | 1 | 0.0167 |
| 5 | 4 | 57 | 1 | 0.0175 |
| 6 | 5 | 58 | 0 | 0.0000 |
| 7 | 6 | 57 | 3 | 0.0526 |
| 8 | 7 | 59 | 1 | 0.0169 |
| 9 | 8 | 52 | 4 | 0.0769 |
| 10 | 9 | 55 | 1 | 0.0182 |
| 11 | 10 | 59 | 2 | 0.0339 |

The dialog box for U charts, shown in Figure 10.18, has the same type of flexibility as the dialog box for P charts. You can select the count variable Blemishes and then check the Number of Defects option (so that a Rate variable doesn't even need to be present in the data set), or you can select the Rate variable and then check the Rate of Defects option, as in Figure 10.19.

**10.4 C Charts and U Charts**

**Figure 10.18**

**Dialog Box
for U Chart**

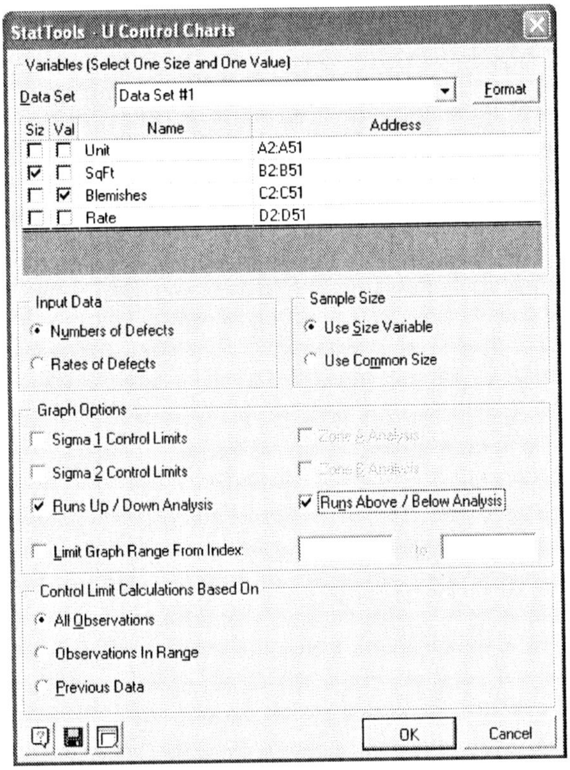

**Figure 10.19**

**Alternative
Dialog Box
Settings for
U Chart**

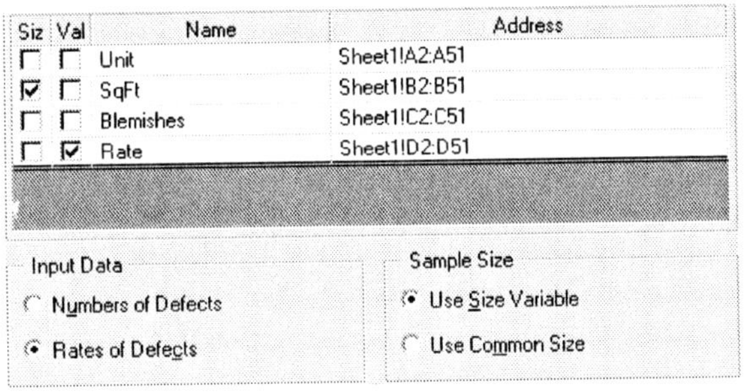

In either case, the resulting U chart, shown in Figure 10.20, graphs the rates through time. Because of the varying sizes of the plates, the control limits are not constant (unless the lower one coincides with the horizontal axis, as in this graph). There is one point that is close to the upper control limit, but otherwise the process appears to be in control.

*Figure 10.20*

*U Chart*

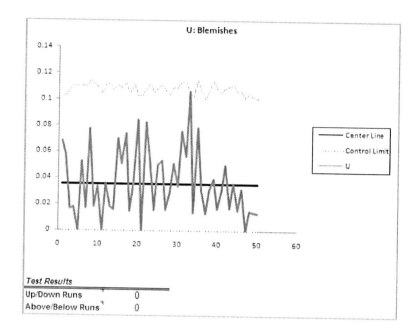

# 10.5 Pareto Charts

The control charts discussed so far are fairly sophisticated tools for tracking a process and seeing when, if ever, it goes out of control. A Pareto chart is a much simpler tool for checking what types of problems a company is experiencing and how frequently they are occurring. It is simply a column chart (and, in StatTools, an accompanying line chart) that shows counts of various problems in decreasing order. That is, it lists the tall bars to the left, so that the company can easily see which problems are occurring most frequently.

To illustrate a Pareto chart, consider the data in Figure 10.21. The data are shown in two ways. Columns A and B list 1000 problems as they occurred through time. (Only the first few are shown in the figure. The full data set is in the file **Pareto Chart.xlsx**.) Columns D and E summarize these problems in a pivot table that shows the counts of the various problems. StatTools can handle either of these data setups.

**Figure 10.21**

**Data for Pareto Chart**

| | A | B | C | D | E |
|---|---|---|---|---|---|
| 1 | Case | Problem | | Problem ▾ | Count |
| 2 | 1 | Out of alignment | | Edge(s) not smooth | 56 |
| 3 | 2 | Holes too small | | Holes in wrong place | 44 |
| 4 | 3 | Paint blemish | | Holes too small | 52 |
| 5 | 4 | Out of alignment | | Out of alignment | 444 |
| 6 | 5 | Edge(s) not smooth | | Paint blemish | 290 |
| 7 | 6 | Out of alignment | | Screw(s) missing | 114 |
| 8 | 7 | Screw(s) missing | | | |
| 9 | 8 | Out of alignment | | | |
| 10 | 9 | Out of alignment | | | |
| 11 | 10 | Paint blemish | | | |

To create a Pareto chart for these data, select **Pareto Chart** from the **Quality Control** dropdown. The resulting dialog box shown in Figure 10.22 has a number of fairly self-explanatory options. First, you can choose one of two Data Types. Select **Category Only** for the data setup in columns A and B, and select **Category and Value** for the data setup in columns D and E. (I chose the former.) Second, for the Category Options, you can add an addition category such as "Other" and you can merge all categories that occur very infrequently.

Figure 10.22

Dialog Box
Settings for
Pareto Chart

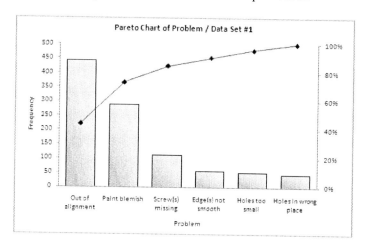

The resulting Pareto chart appears in Figure 10.23. It shows that parts out of alignment and paint blemishes account for the vast majority of problems. The line chart shows the cumulative number of problems (with the scale on the right vertical axis). By the second point, this line is already at about 73%. Such a chart shows the company exactly what it needs to fix in its processes.

Figure 10.23

Pareto Chart

# Chapter 11: Automating and Expanding StatTools

## 11.1 Introduction

To this point, I have described the statistical procedures StatTools can perform. In addition, StatTools allows developers—that is, programmers—to automate StatTools procedures or extend StatTools functionality by writing their own statistical procedures. Both of these are accomplished with **Visual Basic for Applications (VBA)** code. These capabilities require some VBA programming experience, and they require some familiarity with the StatTools programming environment, but the effort can be well worth it.

In this chapter, I will explain briefly what is involved. I will not go into much depth because this material is covered extensively in the StatTools online reference materials. However, I hope to whet your appetite and motivate you to try some of the possibilities.

## 11.2 Automating StatTools Procedures

The StatTools user interface is intuitive and quick, but there might be times when you want to automate a series of tasks without going through the various menu items. Fortunately, this is possible, assuming that you know some VBA. I will illustrate a simple but powerful application in this section. I won't discuss everything in detail, but I will explain the basic steps.

The application is as follows. Suppose you often open spreadsheets that have a data set starting in cell A1. To get a quick feel for the data, you typically (1) define a StatTools data set, (2) create a one-variable summary of selected variables, (3) create histograms of selected variables, and (4) create scatterplots of selected pairs of variables. Wouldn't it be nice if you could click on a button and all of this would happen automatically? This is exactly what my application does. It doesn't include any error checking—it assumes you make reasonable choices—but other than this, it is perfectly general. Assuming you know some VBA (or even if you don't), what do you need to do? Here are the steps.

First, because of the convention I use in my code, you need to do some formatting to the variable name row in your data set: (1) Boldface all variables you want one-variable summaries for; (2) Italicize all variables you want histograms for; and (3) Single-underline all variables you want scatterplots for.

Second, open the Visual Basic Editor (VBE), highlight your data file in the Project Explorer to the left, select the **Tools→References** menu item, and check the two top Palisade items, as shown in Figure 11.1. These items are required so that VBA recognizes the various StatTools functions and objects you use in your code.

*Figure 11.1*

*Setting*
*References*
*to*
*StatTools*
*Libraries*

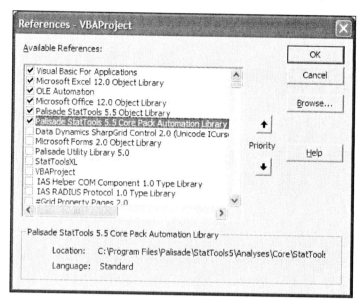

Third, select the **Insert→Module** menu item to insert a module into your project. This module, which is essentially like a blank piece of paper, is where you store your code.

Fourth, copy the following code into your module. I have highlighted the parts that are specific to StatTools for emphasis, but the highlighting is irrelevant otherwise. (In case you have trouble copying from this Word file, where line breaks don't always come through correctly, the macro is also stored in the **Automated Analysis.xlsm** file's module.)

```
Sub QuickAnalysis()
    Dim topCell As Range, dataRange As Range
    Dim ds As StatToolsDataSet
    Dim oneVar As StatTools_OneVarSummary
    Dim hist As StatTools_Histogram
    Dim scat As StatTools_ScatterPlot
    Dim firstScat As Boolean, scatSheet As Worksheet, topScatCell As Range
    Dim i As Integer, j As Integer
    Dim iX As Integer, iY As Integer

    ' Turn off screen updating to prevent flickering.
    Application.ScreenUpdating = False

    ' Assume the data set starts in cell A1.
    Set topCell = ActiveSheet.Range("A1")
    Set dataRange = topCell.CurrentRegion

    ' Create a StatTools data set.
```

```
Set ds = StatTools.DataSets.Add(dataRange, _
    StatToolsVariableLayoutColumns, True)

' Create instances of three StatTools procedures.
Set oneVar = New StatTools_OneVarSummary
Set hist = New StatTools_Histogram
Set scat = New StatTools_ScatterPlot

' By default, put the results in new worksheets.
StatTools.Settings.ReportPlacement = StatToolsPlaceInActiveWorkbook

' Create one-variable summaries for all bold-faced variables.
With oneVar
    For i = 1 To ds.Variables.Count
        If topCell.Offset(0, i - 1).Font.Bold Then
            .VariableList.Add ds.Variables(i)
        End If
    Next
    .GenerateReport
End With

' Create histograms for all italicized variables.
With hist
    For i = 1 To ds.Variables.Count
        If topCell.Offset(0, i - 1).Font.Italic Then
            .VariableList.Add ds.Variables(i)
        End If
    Next
    .GenerateReport
End With

' Create a matrix of scatterplots for all underlined variables.
firstScat = True
iY = 0
With scat
    For i = 1 To ds.Variables.Count
        iX = 0
        If topCell.Offset(0, i - 1).Font.Underline _
                = xlUnderlineStyleSingle Then
            iY = iY + 1
            For j = 1 To ds.Variables.Count
                If topCell.Offset(0, j - 1).Font.Underline _
                        = xlUnderlineStyleSingle Then
                    If i <> j Then
                        iX = iX + 1
                        .XVariableList.Clear
                        .XVariableList.Add ds.Variables(j)
                        .YVariableList.Clear
                        .YVariableList.Add ds.Variables(i)
                        .DisplayCorrelationCoefficient = True
                        If firstScat Then
                            ' Place the first one on a new worksheet.
                            .GenerateReport
                            ' Get ready for the rest.
                            firstScat = False
                            StatTools.Settings.ReportPlacement _
                                = StatToolsPlaceInSpecificCell
                        Else
                            ' Place the rest on the Scatterplot sheet.
                            Set scatSheet = ActiveSheet
                            Set topScatCell = _
                                scatSheet.Range("A7") _
```

```
                                    .Cells((iY - 1) * 21 + 1, _
                                    (iX - 1) * 6 + 1)
                                Set StatTools.Settings _
                                    .ReportDestinationCell = topScatCell
                                    .GenerateReport
                            End If
                        End If
                    End If
                Next
            End If
        Next
    End With

    Application.ScreenUpdating = True
    scatSheet.Range("A1").Select
End Sub
```

Finally, to run this macro, make sure your cursor is somewhere inside the code, and press the F5 key. Everything should appear automatically: the one-variable summary stats, the histograms, and the scatterplots.

Even if you know nothing about the StatTools objects and functions in VBA, you can probably understand what the highlighted lines are doing. In addition, there are two ways to learn more. First, from the StatTools **Help** dropdown, select **Manual** from the **Developer Kit** dropdown. It provides complete online help for programmers. Second, again from the **Help** dropdown, select **Example Spreadsheets**, and open the **Automating Built-In Analysis.xls** file from the **Developer Kit** folder. (Starting with my knowledge of VBA for Excel, it took me less than an hour to learn enough StatTools VBA to write this macro. It is quite straightforward.)

I wrote the above code in a module for a particular data file, but it would be useful to have this macro handy for *any* data file that happens to be open. This is easy to do. Excel creates a **Personal.xlsb** file on your PC the first time you record a macro. This file opens as a hidden file each time you launch Excel, so if you have want some of your favorite macros to always be available, this Personal.xlsb file is the place to store them.

Here is how to do it. First, look in the VB Editor to see whether you already have a Personal.xlsb file in your Project window. If so, you are all set. If not, record any macro. (Do this from Excel's Developer tab. If the Developer tab isn't visible, click on the Office Button, then on Excel Options, and check the **Show Developer tab in the Ribbon** option. When you click on the **Record Macro** button in the Developer ribbon, make sure you store it in your **Personal Macro Workbook**, which is just another name for your Personal.xlsb file. If this file didn't exist before, it will exists after recording the macro.)

Once you have a Personal.xlsb file in the Project window, you can simply copy code, such as the code above, to any of its modules. Then this macro will always be available. However, this particular macro won't function properly until you perform the second step above, that is, until you set the Palisade references through **Tools→Reference** to your Personal.xlsb file. So don't forget to do this.

Once the macro is in your Personal.xlsb file, you can make it even more accessible by creating a button for it on the **Quick Access Toolbar (QAT)** at the top of Excel. This is also easy. Click on the Office Button, then Excel Options, and then **Customize**. On the left dropdown at the top, select **Macros**, choose your macro (such as QuickAnalysis), and click on **Add>>** to add it to the right list. Finally, click on **Modify** and select a suitable icon for your macro. Now your macro is available on the QAT for a one-click analysis of *any* data file that happens to be open! Figure 11.2 shows my QAT at the top with a few custom buttons.

*Figure 11.2*

*Quick
Access
Toolbar*

# 11.3 Developing New Statistical Procedures

Besides automating the statistical procedures that are part of StatTools, you can also create your own statistical procedures and essentially have them become part of StatTools. The programming involved is definitely not as simple as automating existing procedures, but it *is* possible. By the way, the procedures I developed for proportions, slightly modified, are now in StatTools 5.5. In fact, they were discussed in Chapter 5. This section describes the process I used to create them.

You first need to understand the StatTools folder structure. By default, StatTools files are stored under the **C:\Program Files\Palisade\StatTools5** folder. Specifically, StatTools stores a number of add-in files in the **Analyses\Core** subfolder. (See **Error! Reference source not found.**.) For new procedures, you need to create your own subfolder of the Analyses folder. You can name it anything you like, such as My Custom or Joe's Procedures. In my case, I named it **Proportions**, reasoning that this is a good place to store any procedures involving proportions. This Proportions subfolder is where I stored my new procedures for proportions.

*Figure 11.3*

*StatTools Folder Structure*

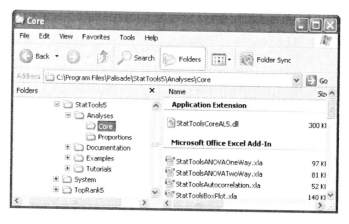

Next, you need to create an **add-in file** that contains your VBA code. Add-in files are special Excel files that have an .xla (or .xlam) extension. To create your own add-in file called **CI_Proportion.xla** (confidence interval for a proportion), open a new workbook in Excel and use the Save As menu item to save it as **CI_Proportion.xla** in the Proportions folder. Note that in the Save As dialog box, you must select the Add-In file type (.xla or .xlam) from the bottom dropdown list.

An .xla file typically stores nothing in its worksheets; it usually contains only VBA code. To see this code, open the Visual Basic Editor, shown in **Error! Reference source not found.**. The list on the left includes the new **CI_Proportion.xla** file. The code goes in modules and user forms, which can be added to the project through the **Insert->Module** and **Insert->UserForm** menu items. I added one of each, and the module with my custom code appears in the figure. Of course, this is the hard part—writing the code—and I will not discuss the details here.

Figure 11.4

Module
Code

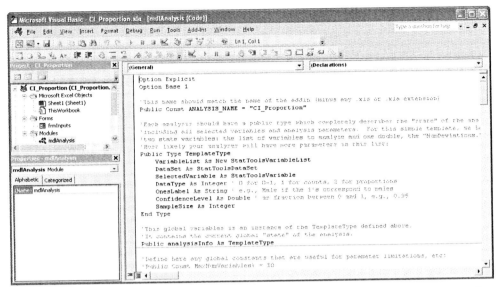

It took me about a day to learn how to use the StatTools tools necessary to develop a new statistical procedure. But StatTools gave me a big head start. First, it provides a file called **Template.xls** (in its Examples\English\Developer Kit folder) that acts as a blueprint for developing new procedures. Second, it provides access to a library of useful VBA functionality. All you have to do is select the **Tools→References** menu item in the VB Editor and check the two Palisade items (Palisade StatTools 5.5 Object Library and Palisade StatTools 5.5 Dialog Controls Library)in Figure 11.5.

Figure 11.5

StatTools
References

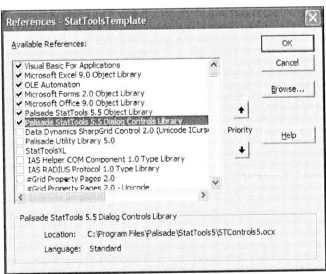

The Dialog Controls Library is particularly useful. It provides two new controls that you can add to the Forms Toolbox for developing user forms. These controls are called STControlsOptionPanel and STControlsVarSelector. (They are the last two at the bottom in Figure 11.6.) To understand why these controls are so useful to a programmer, remember that virtually all of the StatTools dialog boxes look something like the one in Figure 11.7. Specifically, they have a top portion for selecting variables and a bottom left section for various options. If you want your procedure to have a similar look, you don't need to reinvent the wheel. You can simply drag these two StatTools controls to your user form, and with very little effort, they work as they should!

**Figure 11.6**

**New StatTools Controls**

**Figure 11.7**

**Typical StatTools Dialog Box**

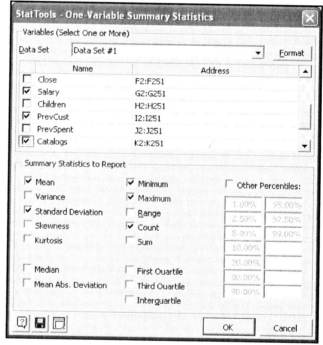

Once the code is written and debugged, there is one more one step to perform. It would be nice if the new procedure would automatically appear in the StatTools ribbon, but it doesn't. The next best thing is to have it appear in the Add-Ins ribbon, and this can be accomplished with a short .xla file. An example appears in the file **CI_Proportion_Menu.xla**. If you load this file, you will see the dropdown in Figure 11.8, where the single menu item is attached to the confidence interval procedure. So even though the new procedure is not a part of the StatTools ribbon, it is still only a click away on the Add-Ins ribbon.

*Figure 11.8*

*New Menu*
*Item*

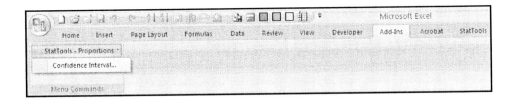

# Index

## —A—

Add-Ins menu item, 5
Analysis Settings, 28
Apply Cell Formatting, 9
Autocorrelation, 149

## —B—

balanced design, 83
Box-Whisker Plots, 54

## —C—

C Charts, 184
chi-square goodness-of-fit test, 91
Chi-Square Independence Test, 87, 88, 89
Confidence Interval for a Mean, 74
Confidence Interval for a Proportion, 76
Confidence Interval for Difference Between Means, 77
Confidence Interval for Difference Between Proportions, 78
Confidence Intervals, 57
    Comparing Two Means, 60
    Paired Samples, 65
    Single Parameter, 57
control limits, 177, 178, 181, 182, 187
Correlation and Covariance, 41
Correlogram, 150
Count Variable, 137
cumulative distribution function, 95

## —D—

Data Set Manager, 8
Data Set Manager Dialog Box, 15
Data Sets Settings, 28
Discriminant Analysis, 139, 140, 141, 143
discriminant function, 141, 142
dummy variables, 109, 110, 111

## —E—

empirical cdf, 95

Exact Linear Relationship, 126

## —F—

Forecast Errors, 157
Forecasting, 153
Forward procedure, 132
full-factorial design, 83

## —G—

Generating Random Samples, 119

## —H—

Histogram bins, 47
Histograms, 45
Holt's Method, 163, 164
Hypothesis tests, 68

## —I—

Importing, 16
    From a Database, 16
    From a Text File, 19
    From the Web, 22
    XML Data, 24
Interaction Variables, 112

## —K—

Kurtosis, 33

## —L—

Lilliefors Test, 95, 96
Loading StatTools, 5
Logistic Regression, 133

## —M—

MAE, 153
MAPE, 153
Mean, 33

Microsoft Access, 16
Microsoft Query, 18
Moving Averages, 154
Multiple Data Sets, 37
Multiple Data Sets in a Workbook, 11
Multiple Ranges in a Data Set, 13

—N—

null hypothesis, 68, 69, 71, 73, 91, 95, 152

—O—

Other Percentiles, 34

—P—

P Charts, 180
Paired-Sample Test, 71, 72, 73
Percentile, 33
Percentile calculation methods, 34
Prediction, 123, 125, 133, 135, 136, 139

—R—

R Charts, 175, 176
Regression, 121, 122, 123, 124, 125, 127, 131, 133, 134, 135, 138, 139
Reports Settings, 27
Residuals, 124
RMSE, 153
Runs Test for Randomness, 151

—S—

Scatterplots, 51

Seasonality, 167
second-order terms, 130
Simple Exponential Smoothing, 159, 160
Skewness, 33
Stacked Data, 36, 49
Standard deviation, 33
statistical distance, 139, 141, 142
StatTools toolbar, 7
StatTools.xla, 5
stepwise method, 127, 128, 129

—T—

Time Series Graphs, 145
transformation, 105
t-statistic, 69, 70, 73
Two-Sample Test, 70
Two-Way ANOVA, 83, 84, 85

—U—

U Charts, 184
Unstacked Format, 104
Utilities Settings, 27

—V—

Variable Names, 12
VBA, 2, 189, 190, 191, 192

—X—

X-Bar Charts, 175
XLA File, 190